The ABC of copyright

The
ABC
of
copyright

unesco

Published in 1981 by the United Nations Educational,
Scientific and Cultural Organization
7 place de Fontenoy, 75700 Paris
Composed by Gerbaud, Paris
Printed by Imprimerie de la Manutention, Mayenne

ISBN 92-3-101889-2

PREFACE

This booklet is intended to provide to all, both near and far, who are concerned with the creation, circulation and transfer of knowledge—authors, educators, researchers, librarians, journalists, broadcasters, producers of phonograms and videograms, producers and distributors of films, publishers, as well as readers among the public at large—replies to certain questions they may have on the subject of copyright.

If there was a time in the past when it was possible to think, as in the Latin expression, *primum vivere, deinde philosophari* (live first and philosophize later), today it is universally acknowledged that social and economic progress depend to a large extent on the existence of people with the necessary knowledge and drive to harness resources to the best advantage in the field of science, technology and administration.

One of the paths to progress—or even to making the best of the present situation—is to develop education and professional training, to encourage research and to disseminate information ever more widely. Works of the mind (works and documents of a pedagogical, scientific, technological or cultural nature) no matter what the medium (print media, audio-visual or computer) play a decisive role in this regard as essential tools of training, information, promotion of culture and entertainment.

It is therefore important for governments to create a climate favourable to national intellectual production and fruitful exchanges between nations. In this effort, effective copyright laws are crucial. But laws and decrees alone cannot accomplish these goals. Recognition by the states of the basic role played by authors' societies in creating a propitious climate for the creation and dissemination of works of the mind is also essential.

Copyright did not drop suddenly from the sky but resulted from a slow evolution. Its history is shown in a sketch in Chapter 1 to elucidate certain developments within a historical context. Questions regarding the origin and nature of copyright have provoked in the past, and still provoke, many controversies.

But even if there is no uniform definition of authors' rights today, the legitimacy of copyright is universally recognized. Copyright law is an integral part of communications and education, and is called upon to play an ever more important role in shaping the process and the great diversity of ways in which copyrighted works are now used: *process* to the extent that the use of literary, scientific and artistic works constitutes an essential element in development; *diversity* resulting from the evolution of modern techniques of diffusion and communication.

In its original structure issuing from the laws of the eighteenth century, copyright was sacrosanct and absolute in theory, monolithic and exclusive. But the evolution of economic, political and social structures linked to science and industrial development prove the possibility, if not the necessity, of the coexistence of several rights: the right of the author in his work with his prerogatives of a pecuniary and moral nature; the right of the public to research, scholarship and knowledge. This coexistence poses the problem of relationships between the owners of copyright and the users, a problem that leads finally to concepts that are complementary.

Thus, the legal policy determining the norms applicable to copyright appears to be intimately linked, on the one hand, to social, economic and political structures and, on the other hand, to the pressures imposed by the development of methods of dissemination of copyrighted works within the context of the contemporary technological revolution. It suffices to mention earth satellites and computers.

In the past, the discovery of printing led to a policy involving primarily producers of works rather than authors. Today industries linked directly or indirectly to the transfer of knowledge require modifications in the legal apparatus which sanctions the transfer of knowledge.

The phenomenon of rapid contemporary change that copyright is called upon to regulate by means of formulating applicable norms has an impact on the creation and transfer of knowledge and information.

The recognition in a country of copyright and the adoption of a national law in this field does not suffice to guarantee the protection of creators. Such laws must be effectively and efficiently applied. It is up to authors' societies and professional associations, as well as government offices and agencies to take adequate measures, because individual initiatives are not enough to assure the protection and defence of intellectual creations. This is true both at national and international levels. Added to this is the fact that users with which authors must negotiate are no longer simply individuals but powerful groups in the face of which authors must be well organized.

Unesco, with its constitutional mandate 'to promote the free flow of ideas by word and image' and 'give the people of all countries access to the printed and published materials produced by any of them by encouraging co-operation among the nations in all branches of intellectual activity' and by 'assuring . . . protection of the world's inheritance of books, works of art and monuments of history and science', has a fundamental mission to encourage intellectual creators through the safeguarding of their professional dignity and economic security so that intellectual creativity may continue as a fertile source of learning, knowledge and progress. Unesco must also see whether certain fundamental principles governing copyright are in harmony with the development of education, science and culture in contemporary society and are likely to satisfy the educational and cultural needs of the international community and in particular the least advantaged within that community. At the same time, it is incumbent on the Unesco Secretariat to see that the legitimate protection of authors does not hinder the dissemination of information or of protected works, specifically those of an educational, scientific or technological nature. From this flows the necessity to make known the role of copyright in determining educational, scientific, cultural and information policies.

This booklet attempts to respond to this need and has no other objective than to clarify a complicated subject by translating legal language into a language that can be easily understood by everyone. Numbers of scholarly works have been written on the subject. But a need has been felt for a copyright primer that would provide an overall view and sum up the essentials of copyright. This explains the approach taken in writing this booklet. It is not a legal or scientific study on copyright but an attempt to provide practical answers to questions that are daily asked in this area.

CONTENTS

1

Copyright past and present

What is the role of copyright in the modern world?

Today we live in a world of instant global communications. Everyone is familiar with the technological developments that have come with dazzling rapidity. In recent decades, techniques for reproducing documents, notably photocopying, have revolutionized the possibilities for quick, easy copying of printed works. New techniques for recording sound and visual images have proliferated almost as fast as the eye can see. Within a century, the world has moved from the daguerrotype to colour television. Television is still evolving, increasing its coverage with hook-ups to earth satellites. The home video machine provides the means to copy television programmes off-air for later use. Simple, inexpensive and readily available magnetic-tape reproduction equipment, coupled with inexpensive cassette tapes, have made it possible to copy phonograph records easily. Computer technology has created a new dimension in communications and information science with prodigious capacity to store and retrieve knowledge.

These technologies are providing unprecedented opportunities for com-munication between peoples. They are also providing new tools for teaching. At the same time, because they all utilize copyrighted works, they are sending shock waves through the legal community because of the oppor-tunities they present for piracy on a large scale. Copyright owners are bringing law suits where unauthorized use is made of their work. They are also seeking new forms of legislative protection. Copyright laws are being revised to meet the challenge of the new technologies.

Seen from this perspective, it is clear that copyright law plays an important role in the complex world of modern communications. It forms the corner-stone of publishing and the legal framework within which other media of communications must develop everywhere. Copyright law provides protec-tion to authors and other creators of works of intellectual creativity, in other words, for the works of their minds. Copyright laws are designed at the same time to encourage the creation and dissemination to the public of original works.

Copyright has always been inseparably linked to technological advance. In the past, new technologies have forced changes in copyright law. Over the years, with the evolution of technology, the number of vehicles for copyrighted works has grown steadily until today the world of copyright comprises a broad spectrum of media of communications ranging from books and magazines to films, radio and television, phonograph records, photo-copying and computers. Today the number of copyrighted works is virtually countless and the commercial values placed on them staggering. Because of the evolution of technology, copyright must now be carefully taken into account by the business world in the structuring of industries and markets. How has this situation come about? It is impossible to have any real under-standing of copyright without taking a look at how the law has evolved over the centuries in response to contemporary needs.

How did copyright begin?

A long complicated history led to the role of copyright in the world today with its far-flung interests. It is a complex story, reflecting mankind's long, groping evolution towards the rule of law in governing public and private affairs. There is not total agreement on the details. For example, the origin of copyright has been linked to the European invention of printing in the fifteenth century. But the technique of printing had existed centuries earlier in China and Korea unknown to Europeans, and the idea of owning the results of intellectual work was recognized in different ways centuries before Johann Gutenberg, the German printer, invented movable type. The inven-tions of printing and engraving in the fifteenth century, by transforming the conditions for dissemination of printed works, mark decisive dates in the history of intellectual property. But ethnographers have put forward the notion that, stretching back to the earliest historical times, there was some notion of literary property.

Before the pecuniary interest of the author in his work was recognized, his moral interest was perceived. In ancient Greece and Rome, plagiarism was condemned as dishonourable and the Greeks were not entirely powerless to repress literary piracy. Studies of Roman literature indicate that authors of the time were not satisfied with glory alone but drew some profit from their manuscripts. Roman authors were aware that publication and use of a work involved intellectual and moral interests. It has been argued by some authorities that the notion of copyright has always existed but it did not find expression in legislation for a long time.

How did Gutenberg change things?

Prior to the era that began with Gutenberg's invention, works of intellectual creation were regulated by the laws of property. The author of a work (manuscript, sculpture or picture) became the proprietor of a material object and he could sell it to another person. In medieval times, it was extremely difficult to multiply a work. A manuscript could only be re-written by hand which severely limited the possible number of copies. Future use of a work would, therefore, not cause damage to the economic interests of the author since his economic interests were not based on the production and dissemination of large numbers of copies of the work. Imitation of sculptures and paintings or plagiarism were rare and severely condemned by public opinion when they did occur.

Books were rare when Gutenberg invented movable type, and printing, as we know it, was introduced to Europe. With the development of the printing press, the costs of manufacturing books decreased and they became more widely available. With this development, a manuscript could be printed and multiplied in a considerable number of copies and distributed to the public. Thus, works of intellectual creation became the object of commerce and could bring benefits to their authors. The first beneficiaries of this new commerce were the printers who were granted the privilege of printing ancient manuscripts. Later, they began printing the works of living authors.

What happened after Gutenberg?

Beginning with the invention of printing, the risks run by 'stationers' increased. (At that time, stationers performed all the activities involved with dissemination of writings—printing, publishing and bookselling, which are separate functions today.) Stationers were required to acquire costly new equipment for printing a great number of copies which sold at relatively low prices at uncertain intervals. Sometimes, long periods of time elapsed before they recovered their costs. Competition also grew, some of it in the form of speculators who printed books already published. Thus, at the end of the fifteenth century, as printing came into its own, piracy of copyrighted works was also born.

Secular rulers and the clergy, both in England and on the continent of Europe, were quick to recognize the importance of these developments. They saw the printing press as a powerful new political and social influence that could threaten their power and began to interest themselves in the distribution of printed works. Sovereigns were thus prompted to grant privileges for a given publication to certain printers. At the same time, the central authorities used the system of printing privileges to control and censor the output of printers and gag the press. From the late fifteenth to the early eighteenth century, the history of printing was marked by the issuance of various royal decrees and statutes granting privileges.

When was the first copyright law enacted?

During the seventeenth century, under the liberalizing influence of the English philosopher John Locke and others, the old order was shaken.

Ideas of individualism emerged and the parliamentary system replaced the absolute monarchy. Restrictions on the printing press were also gradually reduced, and the system of printing monopolies was challenged as a result. In the chaotic situation that followed, in which the system of crown monopolies collapsed, booksellers and printers defended their privileges, referring to the theory of intellectual property.

In England, the Stationers' Company pressed for some kind of copyright protection. On 11 January 1709, a draft bill was introduced in the House of Commons 'for the Encouragement of Learning, by Vesting the Copies of Printed Books in the Authors or Purchasers of such copies during Times therein mentioned'. This draft became the law of 10 April 1710 known as Queen Anne's Statute. It was the first law on copyright in the modern sense of the term and it recognized for the first time the existence of an individual right to protection of a published work.

The Statute of Anne gave the author of already printed books the sole right to reprint them for a period of twenty-one years from the date of enactment of the law. For unpublished books, the term of copyright ran for fourteen years with a proviso that after the expiration of that term, the author, if still living, could renew the term for another fourteen years.

The protection granted in the Statute of Anne was subject to some formalities—namely registration by authors of their works in their own name and deposit of nine copies for universities and libraries.

The Statute of Anne was limited to books. It did not mention other printed matter, engraving or other art forms. It was soon recognized that the 1710 law did not provide sufficient prerogatives to book authors. It was not enough to give an author the right to print and distribute his work. There was the question of public performances, dramatic versions and translations. The English satiric artist Hogarth, victim of piratical copying of his drawings, led a successful move for protection of artists, designers and painters which resulted in the enactment in 1735 of an Engravers' Act.

How did copyright develop?

Gradually in France, the concept of literary property replaced the existing system of privileges. In 1777, Louis XVI issued six decrees establishing printing and publishing on a new basis. These decrees recognized the author's right to publish and sell his work. During the Revolutionary era, several important steps were taken in the evolution of French copyright law. In August 1789, the Constituent Assembly decided to suppress all privileges of individuals, cities and provinces. Authors' and publishers' privileges were carried away in the turmoil. When the dust settled, there was an awareness that the time had come to recognize and sanction authors' rights as not being dependent on arbitrary concessions from public authorities but on the natural order flowing solely from the fact of intellectual creation. A copyright decree adopted in 1791 sanctioned the performing right and that of 1793 established the author's exclusive right of reproduction.

In the United States of America, the first copyright laws of various states preceded both the French and American Revolutions. They were used as a justification for specific protection, 'the most sacred of properties', anticipating the use of such phrases in the Constituent Assembly Debate in France in 1791. The law of the state of Massachusetts of 17 March 1789 providing copyright protection said there was 'no property more peculiarly a man's own than that which is produced by the labour of his mind'.

The need for federal legislation was soon recognized in the United States. The United States Constitution gave the Congress the power 'to promote the progress of science and useful arts by securing for limited times to authors and inventors the exclusive right to their respective *writings* and discoveries'.

The first federal copyright law embodying this Constitutional article, the Copyright Law of 1790, provided protection for books, maps and charts —the two latter a judicial departure from the Constitutional 'writings'. The meaning of 'writings' was further extended by subsequent legislation to cover dramatic performances, photographs, songs and other art forms.

There is no agreed theory as to a time when literary property in the modern sense emerged in Germany. References crop up as early as 1690 to natural law and demands that each one leave aside what is not his. In the eighteenth century, the principle of literary property appears. A Saxon order of 27 February 1686 explicitly recognized the authors' right, while protecting against piracy, books that were acquired by publishers from the writer.

The Prussian Civil Code of 1794 recognized that 'when a King's subject has acquired the right to be a publisher, nobody should infringe that book'. The first federal law was enacted in 1837.

In Denmark and Norway, an ordinance adopted in 1741, and enforced until 1814, granted a perpetual property right to authors and their successors in title.

In Spain under Charles III, in 1762, a law legalized copyright while stipulating that the privilege to print a book would be granted only to 'the one who is its author'.

In Italy, although the privileges system was introduced early, the protection of modern copyright received a legal sanction in several states.

In Russia, the first law on copyright dates from 1830. It was concerned only with literary works. Musical compositions were protected by later laws.

How did international protection come about?

By the early nineteenth century, many states, including some in Latin America, had already enacted national copyright laws, amending them from time to time as required to adjust to new technologies. But this legislation was somewhat fragmentary and the territorial character of the copyright laws remained the same. Copyright protection granted by national laws is effective in principle only within national territories. Development of international relations, cultural exchanges, translation of works into other languages required protection of works of national origin outside national territories and of foreign authors within national boundaries.

Historically, foreign works were originally accorded protection by establishment of special clauses in national laws providing for reciprocity. In other words, if the works of nationals of State A were protected in State B, then works of nationals of State B would be protected in State A. Some bilateral treaties were also concluded. But these measures did not meet the whole problem of international protection. A need was recognized for multilateral international instruments which would oblige contracting states to protect foreign works on a large scale. And the emphasis in copyright law evolution began to shift to the international scene because many authors and artists were suffering from piracy abroad.

At the end of the nineteenth century joint efforts of a number of states led to the conclusion of the first multilateral agreement—the Berne Convention for the Protection of Literary and Artistic Works, which was signed in 1886. In the twentieth century, a number of international conventions were concluded in Latin America. And in 1952, the other major international copyright convention was adopted, the Universal Copyright Convention.

2

An overview
of copyright

What are the underlying principles?

Copyright is based on the premise that no property is more peculiarly the individual's than the products of his or her mind. Copyright is an assertion in law that writers and artists have the right to ownership in their works. They are entitled to protection against unauthorized use of their work as well as a share in any earnings from its use by the public. Copyright, and in some countries other laws, also provide protection for another set of interests, which have come to be called the 'moral rights' of authors. These involve such questions as the right to claim authorship and respect for the essential character or integrity of the work.

But more than that, the rewards that copyright assures the individual creator of artistic, scientific and literary works provides a stimulus to creativity from which all society benefits. In promulgating copyright laws, legislators have recognized the needs of society for access to knowledge. They have therefore attempted to find a balance between the essentially conflicting needs of society for knowledge and learning and the rights of the individual creator.

Have authors endorsed these ideas?

These underlying principles have received endorsement from authors' organizations around the world. The Charter of Authors' Rights, adopted by the International Confederation of Societies of Authors and Composers (CISAC) at a meeting in 1956 attended by representatives of thirty-five countries stated that:

A work of the mind is at one and the same time a manifestation of the author's personality and an economic asset. The author's right over his work is, therefore . . . a right akin to that of paternity. On the same principle, the author is entitled to an exclusive, transmissible right in all forms of economic exploitation of his work, whatever their value and purpose.

At the same time, the CISAC Charter said:

The authors of literary, musical, artistic and scientific works play a spiritual and intellectual role in society which is to the profound and lasting benefit of humanity and a decisive factor in shaping the course of civilization.

The State, accordingly, should grant to the author the widest possible protection, not merely in consideration of his personal achievement, but also in recognition of his contribution to the common good.

Are there different systems of copyright?

Copyright laws differ from country to country because they have attempted to express these general policy objectives according to specific contemporary needs. Different national objectives have dictated different choices or imposed different constraints at different times. But whatever the basis in law, it has been generally recognized that protection is necessary.

There are various systems of national copyright protection but three main branches of copyright law—national laws reflecting the Roman legal tradition, national laws reflecting the Anglo-Saxon legal tradition and national laws reflecting socialist systems.

What is the general nature of copyright protection?

The inventiveness, skill and labour of the creator are protected by copyright. But as a practical matter, this creativity cannot be protected until it has been expressed in a form. Copyright protects original works of intellectual creation in the fields of art, music, science and literature.

The works themselves are protected, the form or manner of expression —not the author's ideas. Ideas, systems, principles and methods may not be copyrighted. There must be an expression of an idea in a material form such as a book, magazine, painting, musical composition, choreograph, film or phonograph record. Unauthorized copying of the work is tantamount to theft.

Generally, on the national level, copyright protects the creations of nationals of one state within its borders or works first published in that state. Copyright laws protect literary, artistic and scientific works in various forms, define the beneficiaries of protection and define the scope and duration of this protection. Multilateral conventions or bilateral treaties extend copyright protection across national boundaries.

Are there other laws that protect creativity?

There are other laws that protect works of the mind. Copyright is one form of what has come to be called intellectual property. Intellectual creations in other fields of human endeavour are not the subject-matter of copyright but may be protected under patent, trademark or design protection laws for industrial drawings.

Copyright finds its justification in fair play and in traditional notions of personal property. And it involves the granting of a monopoly for a limited time to allow creators to earn a living from uses of their work.

Does copyright have a special language?

Copyright law has its own special terminology or jargon which can sometimes be confusing. Words are given precise legal meanings that differ from normal everyday usage. For example, there is the expression 'literary works'. Copyright is said to protect 'literary works' and indeed works of literature such as novels and poems are covered. But so too are musical, scientific and works of the plastic arts. Some laws use the expression 'literary works' to cover all of these. Others use the expression 'literary, artistic and scientific works'. In the case of scientific works, only the literary or artistic expression is protected, not the idea as such.

Use of the word 'author' may also be confusing. In copyright law, the creator of the literary, artistic or scientific work is referred to as the 'author'. But depending on the form of expression, the 'author' may also be a painter, sculptor, composer, choreographer or other artist.

What is originality?

Copyright is a right given to or derived from works. It is not a right in the novelty of ideas. It is based on the right of an author, artist or composer to prevent another person from making unauthorized use of an original work. Two people may arrive independently at the same result and enjoy a copyright in the work if it has not been copied from a previously copyrighted work. An original work is therefore defined as the product of one person's independent thought and labour. Originality is not dependent on novelty or on the artistic merit of the work.

What are protected rights?

Authors' rights lie at the heart of all copyright laws. They involve a clear distinction between the rights of the copyright owner and the rights of someone who owns a physical object such as a book, record or painting. A picture is one thing and the copyright in it is another. The same is true for other works of intellectual creation such as a painting. If a painter sells his picture this implies transfer of the copyright in it only if he has signed a contract so stipulating. In another example, once a copy or recording has been lawfully made, the owner can dispose of the physical object as he sees fit but he cannot duplicate the recording without the permission of the copyright owner.

In other words, the different rights in copyright correspond to the ways in which a work is used. These rights fall into two general categories—reproduction and communication to the public. Both involve many different forms of expression and therefore require the granting of a variety of different rights.

Is the author's permission required?

Since the work of an author is an expression of a characteristic way of thinking, equity requires that he should have the authority to decide whether his work should be made public. Only the original author has the right to reproduce the original article and sell the copies reproduced or grant to others the right to do so. If others could make use of the work without the author's permission, they would illegally profit from the author's skill and labour. The law therefore gives to authors certain exclusive rights for a limited time in relation to so-called literary works. These rights enable the author to share in any earnings from use of his or her work.

As a general rule, these rights are exclusive and use of a work requires the prior authorization of the author. But because of the need to find a balance between the author's personal rights and the needs of society for knowledge and information, the exclusive rights of authors have sometimes been limited by law. In some instances, laws do not grant the owner an exclusive right or authorization but only a right of remuneration. In cases where the law expressly permits use of a work under a compulsory or statutory licence, the owner cannot prohibit use of the work but the user must nevertheless pay for the use.

How do authors benefit economically?

Use of the work by the public is what brings creators their economic return under copyright protection. In order to make a work available to the public, the author may authorize its reproduction, performance or other use. The work may, for example, be published, broadcast, performed on a stage, made into a film, televised, recorded or translated into a different language. Copyright laws affirm that authors should have a reasonable return for their work.

Public acceptance and the conditions of use determine the revenues received by the author for the work of his or her mind. Where copyright laws exist, a percentage of the purchase price of a book, or the admission price for a play is set aside for the author. The money the author receives in this way is called a 'royalty'. The percentage of the royalty fee, and other terms under which the author agrees to the publication or other use, are usually determined in contracts between the author and the user. This royalty system, by which authors are enabled to make a living from the proceeds of the uses of their work, is an essential element in copyright protection.

How does society benefit?

This system of support for authors, enabling them to live on the receipts from public use of their work, permits them to pursue their creative careers. As they win public acceptance for their works, they can concentrate on the full development of their creative energies. Without copyright protection, they would not have the necessary incentive to dedicate themselves to work from which all society benefits. Publishers and other media of communications need a return for their risks and investments in the production, distribution and sale of works. Copyright therefore provides strong encouragement to the search for knowledge and the dissemination of information.

Does technology play a role?

Since the rights granted by copyright reflect the different uses of a work, they necessarily reflect the evolution of communications technology. It is generally conceded that the evolution of modern copyright law began with invention of the printing press in the fifteenth century which made it possible to produce and disseminate copies of literary works on a large scale.

As technology has evolved, these uses have multiplied until today the modern world is bedazzled by an array of contemporary technological developments ranging from phonograph records to radio and television, reprographic reproduction, video tapes, computers and earth satellites. All of these means of communication utilize copyrighted works. The development of each new technology presents new opportunities for creative expression. Each development also presents new possibilities of use, requiring that a new balance be found in the law between the goal of encouraging and rewarding intellectual creativity by protecting works and providing public access to copyrighted material. The process of changing the law to adapt to contemporary realities is continuous and goes on today as it has in the past.

3

The moral right
of authors

Is copyright a human right?

The relationship of human dignity to the arts and sciences and the search for knowledge finds eloquent expression in the Charter of the United Nations and in the Constitution of Unesco, which states that 'the wide diffusion of culture, and the education of humanity . . . are indispensable to the dignity of man and constitute a sacred duty which all nations must fulfil'.

The fundamental theory of copyright is based on the need of mankind to have access to the fruits of knowledge and the corollary necessity to stimulate the search for knowledge by rewarding the searchers. Copyright has thus been accorded a place as a basic human right in the Universal Declaration of Human Rights adopted in 1948 by the General Assembly of the United Nations. It makes this assertion in Article 27:

(1) Everyone has the right freely to participate in the culture of the community, to enjoy the arts and to share in scientific advancement and its benefits.

(2) Everyone has the right to the protection of the moral and material interests resulting from any scientific, literary or artistic production of which he is the author.

What is the moral right of authors?

The author's work is a source of material support. He has an economic interest in its publication, presentation, communication to the public or adaptation. At the same time, the author is said to 'live in his work'. As a creation of the mind, intellectual property reflects the author's personality. It is part of the human personality and therefore something to be valued more highly than the physical property that exists outside the personality.

The term that has been given to this second non-pecuniary interest is 'moral right'. It involves such questions as whether a work should be made public at all, the integrity and inviolability of the work. But the term 'moral right' is misleading to a certain extent because it seems to imply that these rights cannot be legally enforced. In fact, both sets of interests, the moral and the economic, are enforceable by legal means. Also, the term 'moral right' does not mean that the right has no economic importance.

How are moral rights recognized?

The moral rights of authors find expression in the copyright laws of many countries, especially those of the Roman legal tradition and socialist systems. In many countries, they have developed through court decisions.

In Anglo-Saxon countries, these basic rights are protected under general principles of law. For example, in the United States of America, where the moral right is not recognized in copyright law, the basic moral rights are recognized in civil and penal law, laws on unfair competition, contracts, defamation or the right of privacy. Pressure for recognition of moral rights has built up in recent decades because new means or forms of reproduction or diffusion, such as radio, films and television, have seriously threatened them. Increasingly, these rights are being established but there is still discussion of their juristic basis.

Does the author have the right of secrecy?

The author's most fundamental moral right is his interest in controlling publication or presentation of his work to the public. It is generally recognized that the work remains the author's secret until he chooses to divulge it. The right to disclose or make the work public is therefore the basis for all other rights granted by law. The author has the right to decide when and in what manner and under what conditions, his work will be made public.

In most laws, this right is recognized simply as the right 'to publish'. (In this, moral and economic rights overlap as they frequently do.) But in some laws, the question is viewed in a more general way as the 'right to make the work public'. This right is established in such terms as: 'the author has the right to determine whether and how his work is to be disseminated'; 'the author has the right to decide on the publication of his work and on the first public communication of its essential content'; 'it shall be the right of the author to decide whether his work may be made available to the public'.

What is the right of authorship?

This is the right of an author to claim recognition for his work and to associate or not associate his name with it. The right to the name means that the author may communicate his work to the public under his own or borrowed name (pseudonym) or anonymously. He may also want his name to be mentioned every time a work is used in printed or published copies, announced in the case of public performance, broadcast or used in quotations from his work. Also involved is the right to prohibit the alteration of his name or use of his name in connection with the work of another author. The individual may also claim recognition as the author of a particular work as in a case of plagiarism when another person falsely claims authorship.

Does the author have control after publication?

It sometimes happens that after a work is published with the consent of the author, his ideas change and the work no longer reflects his intellectual or artistic views. In such cases, some laws accord him the right to withdraw his work from circulation, modify it or decide on further uses in other forms. When a work is withdrawn from circulation the author may have to indemnify the publisher for losses sustained as a result. Also, in some laws, if the author wishes to put the book back on the market, he must give the book to the same publisher if the publisher so wishes.

Some laws give the author the right to make corrections or improvements in his work when a new edition is prepared. In certain laws, this right is subject to the condition that the corrections or changes must not alter the original aim and character of the work or involve undue expense for the publisher.

Can the author control the integrity of his work?

Since his personality and reputation are intimately bound up with his work, it is in the author's interest that he should be able to prevent any distortion, mutilation or derogatory action in relation to it that would be prejudicial to his honour or reputation. This right has been called 'the right to respect' for the work for its essential character or originality.

The author may move to restrain use of his work or claim damages on these grounds. As an example of how this right may be exercised, if a publisher wants to make changes in the work that he considers reasonable to meet certain editorial standards, if he wishes to make an abridgement or include a short work in an anthology, he is obliged to obtain the consent of the author. No one has the right to modify either the form or the contents of the work without the consent of the author. Sometimes, the author is also granted the right to defend himself against abusive criticism.

How long do moral rights last?

In countries where the copyright laws expressly recognize moral rights, authors retain these rights even after the author's economic rights have been transferred. The Roman legal approach is generally to regard moral rights as perpetual and inalienable. When they are recognized in copyright legislation following the Anglo-Saxon tradition, they are usually of limited duration specified in the law, failing which they lapse on the death of the author. Conditions for the exercise of these rights are also spelled out in the law.

In some countries, these rights are unassignable and, after the death of the author, they are exercised by his heirs regardless of ownership of the economic rights. When there are no heirs, the moral rights, under certain laws, may be exercised by a competent authority appointed for that purpose. And in some legislations, the moral right, after the death of the author, becomes an obligation of fidelity to the author's wishes with regard to publication.

4

Economic rights
of authors

Economic rights for what?

Broadly speaking, the economic rights of the author are those that enable him to earn a living from his work. The revenues the author receives are simply payment for the work of his mind. All copyright laws reflect the guiding principle that the author is entitled to a reasonable share of the economic returns from public use of his work. This principle weaves like an unbroken thread through the entire fabric of copyright law.

What is the nature of economic rights?

Laws designed to protect authors' rights involve an intricate interaction between moral and economic elements, posing special problems for legislators. But it has become customary to distinguish between two sets of rights—the so-called moral rights of authors described in the previous chapter, and their economic rights. To a certain extent the two sets of rights overlap and they are not always easily distinguishable, as for example, in the basic moral right of disclosure or first publication. The economic rights are the more narrowly pecuniary prerogatives inherent in copyright.

Economic rights generally correspond to the different ways in which a work may be used. They reflect communications technology, and the number of authors' specific rights has increased over the years with the evolution of technology. The extent of the author's reward depends on public acceptance of his work and the conditions of utilization.

One fundamental feature of modern copyright law is the exclusivity of these rights. With some exceptions, they are exclusive in the sense that only the author may authorize each use. Each right may be owned and enforced separately and the author's consent is required for each use corresponding to each right. The Anglo-Saxon legal approach insists that the author's control relates only to the whole work or a 'substantial part' of it.

How have these rights evolved?

In the English-speaking world, the term 'copyright' originated at a time when copying was practically the only means of deriving economic benefit from the work of an author. The term 'copyright' was appropriate to describe the author's right to control copying of books or other printed material. But the term is no longer descriptive in the literal sense because it now embodies a much broader notion, including the right to communicate to the public and public performance. With each new technological innovation, the prerogatives accorded to authors and other creators have expanded. The Germans use a more appropriate term, *'Urheberrecht'*, meaning the right of authors. And the French employ the equivalent *'droit d'auteur'*.

In recent times, the courts and legislators have struggled with the conflicting goals of protecting the rights of authors while advancing the dissemination of knowledge. The basic legislative problem is how to find ways to provide the necessary monetary incentives to write, publish and disseminate creative works while guarding against the danger that these works will not be disseminated as widely as they should because of the legitimate rights of authors.

How do national laws grant economic rights?

Different approaches have been followed in granting these rights. Some laws, notably those dating from the early part of this century, entitle the author to a general right of exploitation, disposition or control of a work without specifying the means of utilization. Other laws, instead of proclaiming any particular economic right, specify in varying degrees the different ways a work may be utilized for which the author's consent must be obtained. Examples would be reproduction by various processes, public performance, broadcasting and translation. Laws based on the Anglo-Saxon legal tradition usually define copyright as the exclusive right to act or authorize others to act in ways expressly specified in the law in relation to various kinds of protected works. Finally, there are laws that list particular rights.

What are the basic economic rights?

The author of a protected work has the exclusive right to authorize a variety of acts that fall into two broad categories, (a) the right to reproduce the work and (b) the right to communicate the work to the public.

These rights will be discussed in this and subsequent chapters, notably Chapter 7.

What is the right of reproduction?

Perhaps the most fundamental right granted by copyright laws is the right of the author to authorize the making of copies of his work. Reproduction now involves many separate rights deriving from a multiplicity of methods ranging from printing to engraving, lithography, photocopying and photography to making films and phonograms.

The right of disclosure or first publication, the basic moral right discussed in the last chapter, is closely linked to the right of reproduction. When the author authorizes the reproduction of a work, he settles the conditions under which reproduced copies will be published.

What about distribution?

Sometimes, the right of reproduction includes the right to put a work into circulation or the right of distribution. Sometimes, these rights are protected jointly, sometimes separately.

The right of distribution is also often considered implicit in the right of reproduction. When making a contract for reproduction of his work, the author has the power to define the terms and conditions of distribution of copies. These contracts cover such questions as quantity, price and geographical area of authorized distribution. This right is sometimes written expressly into the law so that it may be exercised separately. Specific mention of distribution may be advantageous for the author in regard to new distribution techniques such as cable television.

What is the right of communication to the public?

This right involves the performance of a work in a public place outside the family or group of friends or acquaintances or the reception of a work by the public. For some kinds of works this has become the most important economic right. It applies to works that may be publicly performed, literary, dramatic, musical works or works of visual art, motion pictures and other audio-visual works, phonorecords or choreographic works.

Performance has a broad definition, covering a wide span of activities from public recitation of a speech or poem, to the playing of a musical work, the exhibition of a painting or sculpture, the broadcasting of a work by radio or television, the playing of phonograph records, the showing of a motion picture, filmstrip or slides, transmission by loudspeaker, cable television, microwave or satellites.

How do copyright laws deal with economic rights?

The best way to answer this question is to give an actual example of the relevant sections of a contemporary copyright law. One such example of a modern law listing particular rights is that of the Federal Republic of Germany. The relevant chapters of that law, dated 9 September 1965 as amended 2 March 1974, read as follows:

3. *Exploitation rights*

Article 15. General—(1) The author shall have the exclusive right to exploit his work in material form; the right shall comprise in particular:
1. the right of reproduction (Article 16);
2. the right of distribution (Article 17);
3. the right of exhibition (Article 18).

(2) The author shall further have the exclusive right to publicly communicate his work in non-material form (right of publicly communicating); the right shall comprise in particular:
1. the right of recitation, performance, representation and presentation (Article 19);
2. the right of broadcasting (Article 20);
3. the right of communicating the work by means of sound or visual records (Article 21);
4. the right of communicating broadcasts (Article 22).

(3) The communication of a work shall be public if it is intended for a number of persons, unless such persons form a clearly defined group and are interconnected personally by mutual relations or by a relationship to the organizer.

Article 16. Right of Reproduction—(1) The right of reproduction shall be the right to make copies of the work, irrespective of method or number.

(2) The fixation of the work on devices which permit the repeated communication of a series of images or sounds (sound or visual records) shall also constitute a reproduction of the work, irrespective of whether the objective is to record a communication of the work in visual or audio form, or to transfer the work from one such sound or visual record to another.

Article 17. Right of Distribution—(1) The right of distribution shall be the right to offer to the public or to place in circulation the original work or copies thereof.

(2) If the original work or copies thereof have been distributed through sales thereof with the consent of the owner of the right of distributing the work for the area within the jurisdiction of this Act, their further distribution shall be permissible.

Article 18. Right of Exhibition—The right of exhibition shall be the right to place on public view the original work or copies of an unpublished artistic work or of an unpublished photographic work.

Article 19. Right of Recitation, Performance, Representation and Presentation—(1) The right of recitation is the right of publicly presenting a literary work, by a personal rendition.

(2) The right of performance or representation is the right of publicly presenting a musical work, by a personal rendition, or to perform the work publicly on the stage.

(3) The rights of recitation, performance and representation include the right to engage in recitations, performances and representations perceptible to the public by screen, loudspeaker, or by analogous technical devices, in a place other than that in which the personal rendition takes place.

(4) The right of presentation is the right to make an artistic work, a photographic work, a cinematographic work, or illustrations of a scientific or technical character perceptible to the public by means of technical devices. The right of presentation does not include the right of publicly communicating the broadcast presentation of such works (Article 22).

Article 20. Right of Broadcasting—The right of broadcasting is the right to render the work accessible to the public by a wireless broadcast such as a radio or television transmission, or by wire, or by other analogous technical devices.

Article 21. Right of Communication by Means of Visual or Sound Records— The right of communication by visual or sound records is the right to make publicly perceptible recitations, representations, or performances, of the work fixed on visual or sound records. Article 19, paragraph (3), is applicable by analogy.

Article 22. Right of Communication of Broadcasts—The right of communicating broadcasts is the right to make such broadcasts publicly perceptible either visually or audibly by means of a screen, loudspeaker or analogous technical devices. Article 19, paragraph (3), is applicable by analogy.

Article 23. Adaptations and Transformations—Adaptations or other transformations of a work may be published or exploited only with the consent of the author of the adapted or transformed work. Furthermore, in the case of cinematographic adaptations of a work, or of the execution of plans and sketches of an artistic work, or of copies of an architectural work, the creation of such adaptation or transformation shall require the author's consent. . . .

4. *Other rights of the author*

Article 25. Access to Copies of the Work—(1) The author may demand of the possessor of the original or of a copy of his work that he be allowed access to the original or the copy, provided this is necessary for the making of reproductions or adaptations of the work and does not militate against lawful interests of the possessor.

(2) The possessor shall not be required to deliver up the original or the copy to the author.

Article 26. *Droit de Suite*—(1) Should the original of an artistic work be resold and should such resale involve an art dealer or auctioneer as purchaser, vendor or agent, the vendor shall pay the author a participation at the rate of five per cent of the sale price. There shall be no such obligation if the sale price is less than one hundred German marks. . . .[1]

1. The *droit de suite,* another type of right altogether, has been adopted in some countries in order to give the authors of graphic or plastic works (paintings, sculpture) a share in the proceeds from the public resale of original works which have increased in value since their first sale. The artist or his heirs receive a certain percentage of the resale price ranging from 5 to 20 per cent under different laws.

5

Protected works

What does copyright protect?

Copyright protects authors, but as a practical matter it is the 'works' of the author that are protected. Copyright protects works as forms of expression rather than authors as creators of certain types of works. Moral and economic rights refer to rights in certain works. It is therefore logical to ask what works. Generally speaking, the answer to this question is: intellectual creations in the fields of literature, music, art and science. The authors of the works are the beneficiaries of this protection. What is protected is the expression of the author's ideas rather than the ideas themselves. For example, if an author writes an article on how to build a boat, his copyright will be in the article and it will protect the author against the making and selling of copies of the article by anyone else without his consent. Copyright protection will not, however, prevent anyone from using the ideas in the article to build a boat.

What are the criteria for copyright eligibility?

Copyright laws do not define the criteria for copyright protection but set down several guiding principles—some negative and some positive in character—on the basis of which the courts decide, on a case-by-case basis, whether these principles have been applied. It is up to the courts to draw the fine lines. Their opinions serve as guidelines.

The negative aspects deal with what is *not* required for copyright protection. Works are eligible for copyright protection regardless of the art form, the manner of expression, the quality, purpose or destination of the work. As to the art form, musical as well as literary works and works of the plastic or visual arts may be copyrighted. Works may be communicated to the public in either written or oral form. Quality, novelty or ingenuity are not relevant. Even if a work is strongly criticized for its contents and condemned for its style by critics, specialists and the general public, it will not lose its copyright protection. Whether the work has a cultural value or is essentially utilitarian is beside the point. So also is the purpose or destination. A copyrighted work may explain the functioning of a household gadget or expose an esoteric philosophical theory. In the eyes of the law, both have the right to protection.

On the positive side—meaning that the work *must* contain these elements—a work must be expressed in a form and it must be original. Anglo-Saxon laws often require the additional criterion that works to be copyrighted be fixed in a tangible form. Fixation is not a requirement in laws of the Roman legal tradition which speak only of forms of expression.

Originality in the context of copyright law means that the work must be original in the sense that it has not been copied from another work. It must also represent a considerable amount of creative authorship. The courts do not attempt to define originality but determine, as cases arise, whether a sufficient degree of originality exists.

How do laws define the subject-matter?

Works protected by national copyright laws and international conventions are works of a literary, scientific or artistic nature. Protection is accorded to scientific works on the understanding that only the 'literary' or 'artistic' expression is protected, not the idea. The scope of these categories is broad and is usually defined in national legislation in very general terms, such as 'intellectual works', 'literary and artistic works', 'all kinds of scientific, literary or artistic works, whatever be the manner of their manifestation' or simply as 'literary works'.

These general terms are often accompanied by lists of examples which are considered illustrative and not limitative. Certain categories appear rather regularly in such lists as, for example, books, magazine articles and other writings, lectures, dramatic or dramatico-musical works, choreographic works, musical works, cinematographic works, drawings, maps, paintings, sculpture and sometimes photographic works. Recent laws also mention works prepared specially for radio or television. Some laws recognize works of national folklore and articles of applied handicraft such as tapestries, which are of special importance in protecting artistic craftsmanship and applied arts in many developing countries.

There has been a trend in recent years towards extending the list of protected works and mentioning the names of protected items specifically. For example, the Brazilian law of 14 December 1973 contains a detailed list as quoted below:

Article 6. Creations of the mind shall be considered intellectual works, regardless of their form of expression, and in particular:
(i)   books, brochures, pamphlets, correspondence and other writings;
(ii) lectures, addresses, sermons and other works of the same nature;
(iii) dramatic and dramatico-musical works;

(iv)   choreographic works and entertainment in dumb show, the acting form of which is fixed in writing or otherwise;

(v)   musical compositions with or without words;

(vi)   cinematographic works and works made by any process analogous to cinematography;

(vii) photographic works and works made by any process analogous to photography provided that, by reason of the choice of subject and the conditions under which they are made, they may be considered artistic creations;

(viii) works of drawing, painting, engraving, sculpture and lithography;

(ix)   illustrations, maps and other similar works;

(x)   plans, sketches and plastic works relating to geography, topography, engineering, architecture, scenography and science;

(xi)   works of applied art, in so far as their artistic value may be dissociated from the industrial character of the object to which they are applied;

(xii) adaptations, translations and other alterations of original works which, provided that they have received prior authorization and do not cause a prejudice to the said original works, represent a new intellectual creation.

Article 7. Without prejudice to the rights of the authors of the component works, collections or compilations such as selected works, miscellanies, anthologies, encyclopedias, dictionaries, newspapers, magazines, collections of legislative texts, orders and administrative, parliamentary or judicial decisions or notices shall be protected as independent intellectual works, when, by reason of the selection and arrangement of their contents, they constitute intellectual creations.[1]

Are derivative works entitled to protection?

Copyright protection is also provided for a long list of works derived from pre-existing works. They are protected as original works since their creation requires some special knowledge and creative effort. The derivative work requires a process of recasting, transforming or adapting the pre-existing work, and the permission of the copyright owner of the original works is required in order to make derivative works. There are two types of derivative works that are generally given copyright protection: (a) translations, adaptations, arrangements and other transformations of works; (b) collections or compilations such as anthologies.

The right to a derivative work does not prejudice the right to the works of which it is compiled. In general, therefore, agreement, not only of the author of the new work but also of the authors of the works used to create it, must be obtained in order to publish a derivative work.

What is an adaptation?

Adaptation involves the preparation of a new work in the same or different

---

1. It should be noted that in certain countries of the Anglo-Saxon legal tradition, there is one copyright for the work incorporated into a phonogram and another for the phonogram itself which belongs to the producer of the phonogram. In countries following the Roman legal tradition, the work incorporated in a phonogram is the only subject of copyright.

form based upon an already existing work. In other words, the work of another author is employed as the foundation of a new creation. The new work, as in the case of the film adaptation of a novel or a stage musical play based on a novel, requires special knowledge and skill and an intellectual effort that gives originality to the work, thus making it eligible for copyright protection. Musical arrangements, dramatizations, film versions, sound recordings, art reproductions and condensations are all examples of adaptations. Textbooks written and published in industrialized nations are also sometimes adapted, by changing or making additions to the text, for use in developing countries under a grant of copyright.

How are translations considered?

A translation is also based on a pre-existing work, differing from adaptation in that the objective is to remain as faithful to the original as possible in another language. A translator brings a special skill to his task and often knowledge, not only of the two languages involved, but of the subject matter of the material to be translated. The copyright of the translator or adaptor does not prejudice the copyright of the author of the original work. For the utilization of a translation or adaptation it is therefore necessary to obtain the agreement of both the author of the original work and the author of the translation or adaptation.

Why are collections and compilations protected?

Collections and compilations bring together in one work contributions from different authors for a specific purpose or according to a certain plan and thus constitute new works. An anthology of poems or short stories would be an example. In these cases, the anthology or encyclopedia (if composed of already existing works) is considered as a new work provided the selection and arrangement of the contents are original. National laws generally stipulate that such works are protected only if they have involved intellectual creativity in the editing and arrangement.

6

Limits to copyright protection

Are there limits to copyright protection?

For the social policy reasons already described—namely, the needs of society for access to knowledge and information on the events of the world—the grant of copyright protection is limited.

Since the author has the choice whether to make a work public in the first place, there are no exceptions to copyright protection in unpublished works. But once a work has been published or otherwise communicated to the public, the exclusive rights of the copyright owner are subject to some limits. Copyright may not apply to some works. In all countries, there are works that have fallen into the public domain because the term of copyright protection has expired (see Chapter 9). And in particular cases, under certain conditions spelled out in copyright laws, a copyrighted work may be used without the copyright owner's consent. The grant of copyright is a limited monopoly—limited in the scope of the rights granted and limited in terms of time.

How is protection limited?

In addition to works that have fallen into the public domain because the term of copyright has expired, there are two general categories of works that are not protected for reasons of public interest. They are official acts (and in some cases government documents) and the news of the day. Use of these works is discussed in the two following questions.

Some limits or restrictions are also imposed on copyright protection in the sense that some uses of protected works are permitted without the author's consent. Sometimes, in these cases, payment is required, sometimes not. These limits on copyright have been accepted out of a need to balance the public's interest in access to science and the arts with the rights of authors.

These latter are specific exceptions to the principle that no person may reproduce, communicate to the public or otherwise utilize a work of which he is not the author. Exceptions to the exclusive rights of authors find justification not in the contents of the work but in the intended purpose of the person who uses the work without the author's consent. It is the purpose for which the reproduction, copy or communication to the public is made which justifies the exemption from the writer's or artist's consent.

These exceptions or limits to copyright are found in laws of the Roman legal tradition. In laws of the Anglo-Saxon tradition, more or less the same exceptions are accepted under a concept that has been called 'fair use' or 'fair dealing'. It is a concept that defies precise definition but has been accepted and described by the courts.

Several questions are taken into account by the courts when considering cases of uses under these exceptions. They include the amount and substantiality of the portion used in relation to the entire work, the purpose and character of the use (whether commercial or non-profit), the nature of the copyrighted work and the effect of the use on the potential market or value of the copyrighted work.

These restrictions concern primarily works that the public should be allowed to use freely under certain conditions to further public policy objectives of mass communication, criticism or education. These exceptions apply to: private and/or free communication; copies or reproduction strictly reserved for private use; quotations; instructional use; archives and libraries; permanent monuments or works situated in public buildings.

How are justice and the government served?

The requirements of justice, law enforcement and the functioning of government have been universally recognized by copyright laws. Generally, such official texts as laws and decisions of courts and administrative bodies are precluded from protection. Certain laws also exempt speeches made during legal proceedings, parliamentary or other public pronouncements. Works in which copyright subsists may normally also be introduced in court without the authorization of the copyright owner. And in some countries, namely of the Anglo-Saxon legal tradition, because of the recognized need of people for information about the activities of government, no documents or publications produced by the government may be copyrighted.

Is free flow of news encouraged?

Certain exceptions to copyright protection have long been accepted in order to encourage the public circulation of information and news. News of the day published, broadcast or publicly communicated is not protected. In addition, a number of domestic laws contain a provision that the news media may use protected works or parts of a work on the occasion of a news report. The person who makes the report has no intention of reproducing the work seen or heard incidentally during the news event but only to report the event with which it is connected. News reports made by means of photography, cinematography, newspapers, magazines, radio and television all benefit from this exception which stipulates that use of the protected work must be incidental, accidental or accessory to the information purpose of the news report. It is natural that the author's permission in such cases does not have to be requested.

Another common exception to copyright intended to favour the press permits the news media to publish reports of events of public interest. The author is not allowed to prohibit diffusion of articles on current political, economic or religious topics by the press or by news broadcasts. The notion of 'news articles on political issues' contrasts with that of mere news events, the first involving 'works' and the second impersonal reports of the facts. This rule is never applicable to articles which do not relate to an economic, political or religious subject of a polemical nature. Some laws mention 'press reports' which consist of compilations of extracts from articles in newspapers or periodicals. Reproduction by the press or radio of news articles is generally free except when the article contains an express indication that it is prohibited or the law provides for express notice of reservation of rights. The source must also be clearly indicated. This protects both the periodical from which the extract is taken and the author of the article.

Most laws also exclude from protection certain oral works such as political speeches and speeches made in courts of law by judges or counsel which may be reproduced by the press and transmitted to the public by radio or television on condition that their use is justified as essential to the objective of informing the public of the events of the day.

Are there limits favouring communication to the public?

Various provisions allow communication to the public without the author's consent for one purpose or another. A great number of domestic laws accept this in the case of private and/or free performances, educational activities or religious services. Several countries, for example, allow performances of musical works, and more rarely, literary or dramatic works without authorization for such purposes.

The distinction between private and public use, profit or non-profit use raises problems of interpretation both for communication to the public and reproduction of works. The expression 'personal and private use' is interpreted with varying degrees of restrictiveness. In the case of radio broadcasting, for example, it can be 'free of charge' but never 'private'. In many countries, it is left to the courts, as cases arise, to decide these questions. Nevertheless, there exists today a restrictive tendency with regard to the concept of private use. In some recently enacted domestic laws, this limitation on copyright occurs only in the case of representations that are private, free of charge and take place in the family circle.

What are the rules for quotations?

The right of free quotation is provided for by almost all domestic laws. Passages may be taken from news articles or books, newspapers, films, sound or visual recordings and they may be reproduced word-for-word in the same media of communication. Such quotations are not justified by the contents or the destination of the work but by the intended purpose of the person who wishes to reproduce textually one or several passages of a work. Quotations should be subordinate to a work and serve to illustrate or give added force to a point, convince, criticize or teach. They may also be used for news purposes as already mentioned.

To be lawful, quotations must be limited to uses specified in the law. In regard to different art forms, these are the generally accepted rules:

In literature, quotations may only be made of extracts and they must be short and not replace the original.

In the plastic arts, quotations mean graphic reproductions of all or part of a work of art in a work written for the purpose of illustrating or giving examples. This reproduction is lawful provided that the picture is incorporated into the rest of the work, cannot be separated from it and is not usable or has no value outside the text.

In music, quotations are made in the form of an insertion—in a literary work of a didactic or critical character—of one or more passages of a composition for the purpose of documentation or argumentation.

Are there special provisions for education?

What is involved here essentially is an extension of the right to quote. In the field of education, authors and producers of educational materials and the users of same—students, teachers and libraries—find themselves in conflict frequently over the permissible limits of free use of protected works or portions thereof. Efforts to reconcile these conflicts have been intensified in recent years with the development of new means to communicate or make copies. Limits on exclusive rights of communication to the public and reproduction are both involved in special provisions for educational uses of protected works. The scholarly and copyright communities (namely, authors' societies and publishers' associations) representing opposing interests, have attempted to work out compromise solutions and voluntary guidelines for teachers and classroom and other instructional uses of photocopies of print materials and music as well as sound and/or visual works. The permissible limits of photocopying and off-the-air taping of television programmes, even for non-profit educational uses, have not yet been clearly established. Cases are pending in the courts involving such educational uses.

The essential idea is that anyone may make copies of works they need exclusively for their own personal use when monetary gain is not involved. A case in point is when a student copies a text for personal research or studies. This is a limited use for educational purposes.

Furthermore, as a general rule, some free use of excerpts from published works, broadcasts, sound or visual recordings is permitted in educational institutions and professional training. There may or may not be a stipulation in the laws regarding the length of excerpts. Solutions to this problem found in some laws include such rules as these: (a) use of the work is permitted only after expiration of a prescribed period from the date of the publication of the work without specifying the length of the excerpts; (b) only some brief passages of the same author may be used; (c) the length is strictly defined— for example, at not more than 1,000 words of a literary work or eight bars of a musical work.

Is copying by archives and libraries permitted?

Archives and libraries ensure the preservation of works deposited there and make them available to the public for research and general educational and cultural purposes. Photographic copying, known technically as reprography, has made it possible to produce copies of rare works or manuscripts and documents of all kinds at a low cost. These copies may either be kept permanently in libraries or archives as reference copies or supplied to other persons. Photoduplication has come to play a prominent role in the activities of these institutions in the conservation of collections and the rational organization of loan services. Because archives, public libraries, non-commercial documentation centres and scientific and educational institutions provide a valuable public service, certain laws incorporate special provisions for copying by such institutions. But such copying is strictly limited. The number of copies may be designated and they may be supplied only to persons who are able to prove that they need them for personal study or research. Control of copies given to third persons is difficult. Some collective contracts between the representatives of authors and libraries have been concluded. The question is also currently being considered by legislatures and litigated in the courts since photocopying on a large scale may prejudice the interests of authors when it becomes a substitute for the purchase of the work and erodes the market for publishers. Many laws grant the privilege of photoduplication only for works lawfully made accessible to the public.

May public works of art be reproduced?

One universal limit to copyright protection permits the reproduction of works of art, monuments and buildings permanently located in public places without the author's permission. Justification for this exception is the publicity these works receive. If not permanently situated in a public place, their inclusion in a film or television broadcast is permitted only if it is by way of background or incidental to the main subject. Permission must be sought and royalty fees paid if works temporarily shown are to be reproduced in books or made the central theme of a commercial film. Some laws also make a distinction between works situated outdoors and those placed inside a building.

Are ephemeral recordings permitted?

In order to facilitate the timing of broadcasts, certain domestic laws permit broadcasting organizations to reproduce the work broadcast in the form of a recording. Such recordings are regarded as a technical tool to schedule programmes at different hours. Ephemeral recordings are lawful only under these conditions: they may be made only with the authorization of the author or the law; the reproduction may not be used for purposes other than a broadcast under terms of the authorization; the reproduction must be destroyed or rendered unusable before the expiration of a fixed period beginning with the day of the first use generally ranging from six months to one year; the reproduction must be made by the broadcasting organization itself by its own technical means and for its own broadcasts. It may only be used by the said organization which cannot transfer, loan, rent or exchange it with another. When such recordings have an exceptional documentary value, one copy may be retained for preservation in official archives.

What are compulsory licences?

In some countries, the general interests of promoting culture have led legislators to set limits on copyright for the benefit of broadcasting activities. Radio and television stations in this case are not subject to the rule that they must seek the copyright holder's permission in advance before using a work. Already, in practice, this permission is not obtained in the case of musical works because the copyright owners exercise their rights through organizations which conclude contracts with broadcasting stations giving them the right to use their repertoire. Some laws provide that a type of work may be used without authorization so long as the owner is remunerated. This may be called a partial restriction on the exclusivity of authors' rights and it is established by laws providing for compulsory or statutory licences.

There are three varieties of compulsory licences: those relating to printed works, recording and radio broadcasting.

Under the system of compulsory licences, the copyright owner is obliged to grant authorizations for use of his work by third parties but usually retains the right to negotiate the terms of the use. When the parties fail to come to an agreement, the amount of the remuneration is fixed by some competent authority. In some states, this is done by civil courts and in others by agencies such as copyright tribunals.

The author's right of translation is also limited by some laws so that works may be more readily available in other languages. Translation and reproduction rights are authorized under compulsory licence by some laws with special rules for developing countries to facilitate their access to copyrighted works. These questions will be further discussed in Chapter 13.

Statutory licences, sometimes called 'legal' licences, are similar to compulsory licences in that a work may be used without the copyright owner's consent subject only to payment of a fee with the difference that the amount is prescribed by a competent authority. The legal licence applies to the right of mechanical reproduction under which royalties are fixed as a percentage of the retail selling price of the recordings. In some states, they are calculated on a numerical basis, a prescribed amount for each playing surface. Usually the royalties resulting from such uses are paid to a body designated for the purpose and that body or society distributes them to the authors concerned in accordance with established rules.

7

Copyright ownership

What is the basic principle of copyright ownership?

It is a well-established principle that copyright ownership in a work belongs in the first instance to the person who created it, namely the author. There are exceptions to this rule, some of which will be spelled out below.

Also, as a general rule, copyright can be transferred (see Chapter 8), and can be inherited by the heirs of the author.

Who is the author?

The definition and interpretation of the term 'author' raises questions resolved in different ways by the domestic laws of different countries. The author, in the simplest and most frequent case, is the natural person who created the work. When this person discloses his or her name, there is no problem of confusion with other people. Nor are there difficulties of proof. Because this idea is so self-evident, some domestic laws do not even make mention of it. Some states have expressly incorporated into their laws the generally accepted presumption of authorship based on the appearance of the author's name or recognized pseudonym or pen-name (*nom de plume*) on the work. The translator or adaptor of a work is deemed to be the author. In this case, his right does not prejudice the right to the original work.

Many states hold that only human beings or natural persons can be the original owners of literary or artistic works. A legal entity can only buy or otherwise acquire the copyright in a work since it lacks the capacity to create a work and therefore cannot figure as an author. This approach is most commonly found in states adhering to the Roman legal tradition.

The laws of certain states, on the other hand, recognize that copyright may belong, in the first instance, to a corporate body or legal entity in contrast to a natural person. This is true primarily in states of the Anglo-Saxon legal tradition. For example, in some countries, a legal entity is deemed to be the author of a work produced by its employees in the course of their work. Among the legal entities that may own copyright under different laws are the state, governmental services or agencies, municipalities, academies, universities and institutes.

What are the rules for works made for hire and commissioned?

Many laws of the Anglo-Saxon legal tradition establish that authorship and copyright in works made for hire, under employment contract or salaried contract, vest originally with the author but are deemed by operation of the law to be transferred to the employer. This principle applies to salaried persons or employed authors who produce works in the normal course of their employment. The basic idea here is that the employer directs, pays for and produces the work and it is therefore the employer who should reap any economic benefits. According to the Roman legal tradition, copyright in a work made for hire belongs to the author unless the employment contract stipulates in writing otherwise.

Similar rules apply to works made under contract, or on commission as the result of a special order. Examples of such commissioned works may include a piece of sculpture, an engraving, a photograph or a portrait commissioned against payment. Sometimes works may be commissioned as a contribution to a collective work. Translations, instructional texts, or parts of a motion picture or other audio-visual works may be considered as works made for hire or commissioned works under contracts so stipulating.

Who owns anonymous works?

Copyright laws generally recognize that for one reason or another a person may want to publish a work without revealing his or her name (anonymously) or under a borrowed or pen-name (pseudonymously). In most states, it is the publisher who exercises copyright in such works. But it should be clearly understood that the publisher is not the real owner of copyright. This is a procedural presumption which entitles him to act to enforce the copyright, as a rule, only until the real author reveals his identity.

Who owns works created by several people?

Two or more persons may collaborate in the creation of a work. They may work in such a way that their contributions are merged and cannot be distinguished within the finished work. Works in which several individuals have collaborated on the component parts linked together into an inseparable unit or whole have been called 'joint works' or 'collaborations'. In such cases, the co-authors are usually considered as co-owners. In general, this means that a person who wants to utilize the work must first obtain the agreement of all the authors.

Some laws make a distinction between joint works and collective or composite works where the contributions are separate and distinguishable in the finished work. These works may be composed entirely of literary material as in the case of periodicals, anthologies and encyclopedias. Or they may involve more than one kind of work, literary and musical, for example. The term composite work is applied to new work for the preparation of which a pre-existing work is incorporated (music written on pre-existing lyrics resulting in a song).

In spite of the fact that the contributions to collective works are separate and discernible, they are usually undertaken on the initiative of one individual or legal entity and put together by someone who plans, arranges, co-ordinates, prepares and publishes the collection. It is generally recognized that, without prejudice to the copyrights in the individual works so assembled, there is a separate copyright in the ensemble. Many laws deal with this point, designating the editor or director of the work as the owner of copyright in the collected work as a whole. Subject to stipulations in the contract, copyright in the individual contributions may, however, belong to the respective creators. In the case where pre-existing work is incorporated with new work, both creators will have copyright in their respective works. Utilization of such works requires the authorization of both of them. Many copyright laws do not make these distinctions clearly but there is a fairly general tendency to establish different rules according to which the various personal contributions can or cannot be distinguished.

How are cinematographic works owned?

Since film-making requires the co-operation of many persons, the parties usually draw up an agreement to cover the question of ownership of the copyright in the resulting cinematographic work. Copyright laws are therefore usually invoked only in the event of default of the contractual agreement.

Depending on whether they follow the Anglo-Saxon or Roman legal traditions, two basic solutions to the question of ownership of the copyright of cinematographic works are found in domestic legislation. In the case of the former, the producer of the film is regarded as holding the copyright in the film. Some laws may, however, also provide for reservations giving the principal collaborators (the author of the scenario or adaptation, the scriptwriter, the composer of the music) the right to utilize or dispose of their respective contributions.

Laws adhering to the Roman legal tradition confer copyright in the film to several persons and there may be either a joint copyright for all of the co-authors or a separate copyright for each of the principal collaborators in his or her own creative contribution. Under this system, if a pre-existing protected work is adapted into a cinematographic work, the author of that work is also considered as one of the authors of the new work. But the producer has the right of commercial exploitation of the film without the consent of the other collaborators since withholding such consent could prevent exploitation of the film.

8

Transfer of copyright

Is copyright transferable?

Copyright laws expressly dealing with moral rights of authors are uniform in recognizing that these rights attach to the person who created a work and are inalienable and imprescriptible. In other words, moral rights are inherent in the author and only the author himself, during his lifetime, may exercise them and cannot transfer this power to any other person.

It is also generally recognized that the authors' economic rights are transferable, that the author may entitle other persons to exercise rights as far as different types of uses of the work are concerned. This may be done for valuable consideration or rights may be transferred gratuitously if the author so desires.

The author of a novel, for example, may enter into a contract with a publisher to have his novel published and may transfer one or more rights. He may also make a simple authorization for a particular use, retaining such rights as those of reproduction, communication to the public, translation and adaptation in which case no transfer is involved.

What general rules apply to transfers?

In states following the Anglo-Saxon legal tradition, copyright is considered to be personal movable property and as such it may be assigned wholly or partially to third parties. The legal consequence of the transfer of copyright by way of assignment is that the assignee becomes the owner of copyright (either in its entirety or in respect of one specific right) and can take actions in his own name, including legal actions against infringers. In other words, rights are divisible and can be contracted away separately as in the case of a variety of so-called subsidiary rights for printed works which have become increasingly important in recent years, such as film rights, paperback book rights and translation rights. Authors always retain all rights not transferred expressly. It is generally recognized that the alienation of the physical object does not imply alienation of the existing copyright in the object. Thus a person who acquires a book, a portrait, a photograph or a statue does not enjoy the right to reproduce it.

Laws of states following the Roman legal tradition consider copyright as exclusive incorporeal property or personal rights since a work emanates from the personality of its creator. Thus, rights cannot be assigned, totally or partially, to a third party as in the case of movable property rights. They can only be licensed. To license means to grant the right to use a work that would otherwise have been unlawful. A licence may be granted as an exclusive or a non-exclusive right. An exclusive licence entitles the licensee to use the work to the exclusion of all other persons (even the author himself) in the manner permitted to him. A non-exclusive licence entitles the licensee to use the work in a defined manner concurrently with the author or with other rightful claimants. As distinct from assignees of rights under the Anglo-Saxon tradition, licensees in some of the Roman law countries must join the copyright owner in legal actions against pirates or plagiarists.

In some states with socialist legal systems, economic rights of the author generally cannot be alienated in favour of third parties except for the use of a work in foreign countries. Inside the country, the third party can again acquire from the author only authorization to use his work in a defined manner and for a limited time. After the approved use of the work has taken place, the author can authorize other persons to use it in the same or different manner. Only the author may take actions against infringers.

Are rights transferred totally or partially?

In the case of total transfer or assignment, the transferee or assignee acquires all the economic rights an author can own in a given work or works and is entitled to exercise them as if he were the author himself. Contracts may cause prejudice to the author's interest if they concern all his work or if they transfer his total rights. Therefore, the majority of laws limit transfers of rights in future works.

Where partial transfers are concerned, a transferee usually acquires only the right to exercise one or more specific right as designated in the contract. For example, the author of a dramatic work may transfer to a theatrical impresario the right to perform his work on stage. Or he may transfer to a publisher the right to publish his dramatic work in book form. In such a situation, the theatrical impresario would not have the right to publish the dramatic work in book form, and the book publisher would not have the right to authorize a stage performance. Such grants may or may not be confined to a specific geographical area.

How are rights transferred?

Transfers of copyright are dealt with in different countries by different branches of the law: civil, commercial or other special laws. Transfers are made contractually and freedom to contract involves a variety of problems and an equal variety of solutions depending, for example, on commercial practices as they vary from place to place. In many countries, in practice, freedom to contract is more or less limited by standard contracts and rules of conduct laid down by authors' societies. Many countries have established such societies because of the difficulty authors have in negotiating rights with users. These societies play an important role in protecting authors' rights and facilitating the exercise of copyright.

Usually a contract for transfer may be concluded in whatever form the parties want. It may be made verbally, for example, but some countries require written contracts for assignment or grant of rights, especially when the transfer is effected for valuable consideration. Some laws require registration of contracts (see Chapter 10). ·

The terms of the contract assigning rights usually cover the period of time for which rights are transferred, an enumeration of the rights transferred, the language or languages, territory for which the work may be used, the royalties to be paid, the responsibility of the parties and the procedure for settlement of possible disputes between the parties. Such contracts are normally concluded and fulfilled in accordance with more general law such as civil law or law of contracts.

Some copyright laws, particularly recent ones, contain special provisions dealing with the rights and duties of the parties under contracts for various kinds of uses. In some states, particularly socialist ones, the parties concerned negotiate on the basis of a standard or model contract for different uses such as publication, public performance or broadcasting. These contracts are approved by various organizations of authors and users and have the force and effect of law. The negotiators can deviate from the terms of the standard contracts on condition that the terms of the resulting contract do not put the author in a less advantageous position than that accorded by law or by the standard contract.

Is there a time-limit on transfers?

In order to give authors a chance to renegotiate contracts for more favourable conditions, some laws limit the period of time during which transfers will be valid. Such limits recognize the fact that writers and artists are often inexperienced or improvident when they make their first sales and are likely to settle for unfavourable terms. If, for example, a publisher has done nothing with a work, a new publisher can be found. Time limits vary greatly from state to state.

Are rights transferred after death?

Since the moral rights of authors are inalienable, third parties, for example, heirs, have an obligation to respect the wishes of the author. The author can grant this power to any person by will. In the absence of a will, the power to assure protection of moral rights is transmitted to his heirs by operation of law. In some states protection of these rights is also assured by organizations of authors or by designated government bodies. This helps to preserve the integrity of works which become part of the national cultural heritage. In certain countries of the Anglo-Saxon legal tradition, which recognize moral rights in the copyright act itself, these rights expire with the death of the author.

The author's economic rights may be transferred after death by will or may pass to his heirs by operation of law as intestate succession. The successors exercise these rights during the term of protection in the same way as the author himself.

9

Duration of protection

Is copyright protection limited in time?

Legislators have been motivated in drafting copyright laws by a desire to encourage national intellectual production by assuring to authors during their lifetime, and to their heirs and successors, the exclusive enjoyment of the fruits of the author's labour. If authors are assured that their works will enjoy legal protection during a given period of time they will tend to produce more works thus enriching the intellectual production of their country. Legislators have recognized that protection constitutes a just and equitable reward for the efforts put forth by authors.

But because lawmakers have wanted to encourage access to protected works, they have limited the duration of rights. Copyright therefore protects economic rights, and sometimes moral rights, for a given period of time. The length of the period, and its starting point, differ from country to country. On the other hand, some countries, recognizing moral rights of authors, consider them perpetual.

How long does copyright protection last?

All laws recognize that the economic rights of authors are protected during the lifetime of the author and for a certain length of time after his or her death. That means that the author of a work is assured that his rights in the work will be guaranteed to him during his lifetime, however long he lives. Recent trends in the field of copyright law favour terms of protection generally ranging from twenty-five to fifty years after the death of the author although some laws accord shorter or longer terms. Copyright laws also provide the author assurance that his successors will enjoy protection for a definite period. Certain laws stipulate that the term of protection after the death of the author will endure for the life of his or her spouse. Detailed rules are sometimes established in respect to descendants of the author and/or successors in title to certain rights. Some laws also provide different periods of protection for works published and not published during the author's lifetime.

How are moral rights treated?

Certain domestic laws of the Roman legal tradition that recognize both moral and economic prerogatives of authors do not expressly pronounce on the duration of moral rights. In such cases, it is understood that there is no time limit on moral rights. As a general rule, laws expressly regulating the duration of protection for moral rights state that they are either unlimited in time or perpetual. These laws normally refer to the right of authorship and the integrity of the work. In other words, independently of the author's economic rights, the author and his successors in title retain the right to claim authorship of the work and to object to any distortion, mutilation or other modification or other derogatory action in relation to his work which would be prejudicial to his honour or reputation. The right to correct or withdraw a work from circulation may only be exercised by the author himself during his lifetime. Some laws adopt the position that moral rights are unassignable and may be exercised after his death only by the author's heirs irrespective of ownership of the economic rights. In the absence of heirs, under some legislations, moral rights may be exercised by a competent authority appointed for this purpose.

Laws in the Anglo-Saxon legal tradition that recognize moral rights in their copyright legislation state that they are of limited duration specified in the law, failing which they lapse at the death of the author. A few laws provide that protection of moral rights subsists only as long as economic rights or for a certain period of years after the author's death.

When does copyright protection begin?

Some copyright laws are silent on this subject and the calculation of periods of protection is frequently governed by the civil, penal or procedural law of various countries. But under many copyright laws, the term of protection is calculated from the death of the author or from some event related to the work, usually first publication. The calculation is not always made from the exact date of that event but from the last day of the year in which it took place or the first day of the following year. The general term of protection may also be counted as from the date of first publication of a work. This is the case in a few countries.

It is easier for potential users to ascertain whether works of a given author are still protected by determining the date of the author's death than to establish when various works were published. Under the system of calculating the term of protection from the date of first publication of the work there is always a risk that protection may cease during the lifetime of the author.

Even in countries where the general rule is to calculate the term from the death of the author, there are usually exceptions for cases where such a calculation would be impractical because the number of authors of a given work is too great or it is uncertain who qualifies as author (in the case of collective works), because the author is not identified (anonymous works), or because the work is first published after the author dies (posthumous works).

How is the term measured for works with several authors?

Laws expressly dealing with the general term of protection in case of works created with the collaboration of two or more authors (joint works) generally take the date of the last surviving co-author's death as the date from which the term of copyright protection must be calculated. In a very few laws, the term is counted from the date of the death of the first deceased co-author.

Are there special terms of protection?

Copyright laws have established special terms of protection for such works as serial publications, anonymous and pseudonymous works and works of legal entities, and sometimes as regards photographic and cinematographic works, phonograms, and radio and television broadcasts. These, too, vary from legislation to legislation.

In the case of anonymous and pseudonymous works, the real name of the author is unknown and for this reason the general term of protection after death cannot be applied. It is impossible to count the period of protection if the date of the death of the author is unknown. Therefore, the rights in these works are usually exercised by the publisher during the period provided for in the law—anywhere from twenty-five to fifty years—counted from the date of the publication of the works. But should the author reveal his identity, the general term of protection will apply.

When the author is not a natural person but a judicial person (legal entity), the general term of protection based on the life of the author cannot be applied. In such cases, the established practice is to calculate the term of protection, ranging from ten to fifty years, from the date of publication of the work. A few laws accord perpetual protection to the rights in the works produced by legal entities.

For photographic works, the laws of a number of states make special provisions regarding the duration of protection of the rights in photographs, usually from ten to fifty years after publication of this kind of work even if the name of the author is known and it is not the work of a legal entity. Many states do not deal with this matter. In those states it may be presumed that the general term of protection is applicable to photographs, calculated at the death of the author.

Certain laws contain special rules for the duration of protection of the rights in films, usually from twenty-five to fifty years. In some states, the term of protection is calculated from the date of publication of ᵗhe film. In others, it is calculated from the date of fulfilment of certain formalities such as registration. In others, the general term of protection calculated from the death of the last-surviving co-author applies.

When a phonogram is copyrighted, the period of protection begins either from the date of manufacture (engraving, registration, manufacturing of original plates) or publication. The duration ranges from ten to fifty years.

Special rules for duration of protection are also sometimes provided for works of a special nature such as translations, craftsmanship and applied arts, choreography and pantomimes, collections, anthologies and dictionaries, maps, ideas for stage decoration, engineering plans, titles, fictitious personalities and slogans.

What happens to works when the term of protection expires?

After the prescribed term of copyright protection has expired or required formalities (see Chapter 10) have not been observed works fall into the public domain and may be used by any person without the author's consent and without remuneration. Once a work has fallen into the public domain, copyright is lost for ever. Certain protections are provided under the concept of moral rights even for works in the public domain in some countries of the Roman legal tradition, although this is a complex and controversial question. Also, the laws of certain states provide for a system known as paying public domain (*domaine public payant*) whereby the users of works in the public domain must pay prescribed fees. These fees are collected by designated authorities, usually state bodies, which dispense them for such purposes as general cultural promotion and financial help to needy authors or their families either directly or through recognized organizations of authors.

10

Copyright formalities

What is the role of formalities in copyright?

Copyright in some countries can be linked to various formalities such as deposit of copyrighted works, registration and copyright notice. The general theory is that the protection of authors' rights should flow automatically from the act of creation and should not be dependent on compliance with any procedures. As soon as a work is created, according to that theory, it is protected without the observance of any formality whatsoever. Nevertheless, in some countries the acquisition of copyright is subject to the fulfilment of certain formalities—one or more of those mentioned above. In countries of the Roman legal tradition, acquisition of copyright is independent of formalities and results purely from the creation of the work. And in other countries, deposit may not be required for the acquisition of copyright but only for its exercise or as an administrative measure. One formality, now almost universal, is copyright notice.

Must copyrighted works be registered?

In some countries, authors are required to make a claim to copyright in each work by registering it. What is registered depends on the person claiming copyright. Registration usually includes filling in a form with such particulars as the name of the author, title of the work, date and place of first publication (if published), name of the publisher, language and other relevant data such as the format, number of pages and number of volumes. These forms are filed in a national register.

In countries that maintain registers, registration may be optional or compulsory. Some countries do not require registration. Registration may be called optional when failure to register does not affect protection. When registration is a condition of protection, it may be called compulsory. In both cases, registration is usually recognized by the courts as prima facie evidence of the truth of the facts recorded. In other words, the facts are considered true unless the contrary is proved in court.

The register is kept by a government office with a name such as 'Copyright Office', 'National Copyright Office' or 'National Registry of Intellectual Property'. Requests for registration are made on prescribed forms often accompanied by deposit of one or more copies of the work being registered. In return, the author will receive a certificate of registration if the conditions of copyright are met. In some states, the payment of a registration fee is required.

Copyright registers are open to public inspection and therefore serve as a public record that can be consulted for a variety of purposes. This is one of the arguments that has been made in favour of maintaining a system of national registration of copyrighted works. Compulsory registration as a condition for copyright protection is gradually disappearing, however, because the international conventions have tended to accept the notion that no formality should stand in the way of authors' rights. The Berne Convention states that copyright protection may not be subject to any formality. The Universal Copyright Convention provides that if any state party to it 'requires as a condition of copyright, compliance with formalities, such as deposit, registration, notice, notarial certificates, payment of fees' (Article III), fulfilment of these formalities cannot be required if the 'copyright notice' (see below) appears on all published copies of the work.

Are deposits required?

In some states where registration is a feature of the copyright law, deposit of a copy of the work is a requirement for registration. A copy of the work or a photocopy of some works such as manuscripts, paintings or engravings must accompany the registration application. This deposit serves the purpose of registration only and should be distinguished from mandatory or legal deposit systems established by the copyright laws of other states. Under this second system of legal deposit, one or more copies of a published work must be deposited with a governmental authority, national or special library designated for the purpose. Failure to comply with this legal deposit requirement makes the individual author responsible for non-compliance but does not affect copyright protection.

In addition to deposits under copyright acts, there is a third kind of deposit which may also be called 'legal deposit'. Certain national legislation, completely independent of copyright considerations, requires deposits of a certain number of copies of new books and other materials. These deposit laws were originally conceived and enforced with the primary objective of controlling publication, and date back to the early history of printing. But such laws have evolved over time into a means of building national library collections and preserving the records of national as well as world culture.

What is copyright notice?

The copyright laws of most states require that some kind of notice be affixed to all copies of a work to inform the public that copyright protection is claimed in the work. In some countries, copyright notice is a condition to obtaining and/or maintaining legal protection for the work. In others, protection is not contingent on notice but its omission is punished by a fine.

The internationally accepted copyright notice, provided for in the Universal Copyright Convention, is composed of three elements: the symbol © (the letter 'C' in a circle, the first letter of the word 'copyright'); the name of the copyright holder; the year of the first publication of the work (see Article III, Universal Copyright Convention). National copyright laws contain other notice requirements such as a symbol or expression, for example, 'all rights reserved', 'copyright', 'copr.', or 'DR' (*derechos reservados* in Spanish) plus the name of the copyright owner, the publisher and/or printer, the date of first publication or the year in which the copyright was registered.

Copyright notice should be placed in a prominent position on the work and should be legible and clear. In the case of books or other printed materials, the title page, or the page immediately following, is the custom, but other prominent positions are accepted.

What are the advantages of copyright notice?

The affixing of a copyright notice on a work by the author at the time of its completion or publication does not place a heavy burden on the author and it has obvious benefits for him. It shows to all concerned that the rights in the work are protected. On the national level, it makes it easy for the copyright proprietor to prove that an infringer knew when he utilized the work that it was protected and that he was therefore engaging in an illegal act.

Since copyrighted works can cross national frontiers easily in this age of worldwide communications, an international symbol of copyright protection has great value. The rights of authors are protected in countries other than their own by means of international conventions (see Chapter 12).

11

Copyright infringement and remedies

How are copyright laws enforced?

Because of the high value placed on the intellectual heritage of mankind and the collective interest in protecting creators, the great majority of states at present consider the breach of an author's exclusive rights as a penal offence. It has generally been recognized that penal sanctions added to civil measures offer a particularly effective means of securing adequate and real protection of copyright. This has prompted almost all legislations to provide for the prosecution of persons infringing the rights of creators of works of the mind.

Authors claiming protection and enforcement of the copyright laws make their claims within national systems with different laws, procedures and law enforcement. Their efforts to protect their rights, therefore, do not have uniform results. Authors do not always know their rights, often suffer from lack of financial resources to protect them, and have difficulties finding their way through the complexities of the law and the procedural complications of certain administrative systems. The results of their efforts to protect their rights are therefore uneven from country to country although some generalizations can be made about what constitutes copyright infringement and available legal remedies.

What is copyright infringement?

As a general rule, except in certain cases prescribed by the law, any use of a protected work is lawful only if proper authorization from the copyright owner is obtained prior to such use. Any act with respect to any exclusive right in a protected work constitutes infringement if authorization has not been obtained from the author or other owner of a particular right in advance. Infringement of copyright in any form is tantamount to theft and is liable to action as with violations of other legal rights.

How do domestic laws deal with infringement?

Domestic copyright laws deal with the question of infringements in various ways. There are laws that condemn all infringements in a very general way using such formulas as 'persons who violate any of the exclusive rights referred to in article . . . shall be deemed to have committed infringement of copyright'. Other laws contain a detailed description of punishable infringements such as 'the following acts shall constitute violations of this law: unauthorized reproduction, public performance, broadcasting of a work'. In some laws the two methods are combined. In some countries the provisions of civil or criminal codes are also applicable in cases of copyright infringement.

What are the different kinds of infringement?

The most common forms of infringement are plagiarism and counterfeiting. Each of them implies one or another type of unauthorized use of works protected by copyright. Plagiarism describes the act of copying another person's writings and passing them off as one's own. Counterfeiting is the unauthorized reproduction, performance or communication by any means.

Two other terms have gained currency in common parlance—piracy and bootlegging. But in those cases the infringement is made *vis-à-vis* the material support of the intellectual work or its containers. Piracy is the unauthorized copying of recorded or printed material and the selling of it surreptitiously. The copying of the jacket or container is sometimes done in such a way that buyers (and sometimes even the original manufacturers) are hoodwinked into accepting them as the original products. The infringement does not directly concern the intellectual work, but the copyright owner is denied his just reward.

Who lodges complaints?

The legislation of most states specifies in detail who may lodge complaints and denunciations in the event of copyright offences. The right of initiative may belong to any individual concerned, exclusively to the injured party, to an association of a legal person or less frequently to the state of which the individual is a national in the case of international breaches.

In some countries, public action in cases of offences against literary property may be initiated by a mere denunciation by any individual whatsoever who claims to have had knowledge of the offence. It is not necessary under such legislations for the injured author or the copyright holder to lodge a complaint. Since the countries that have adopted such a system generally base it on public policy, the public prosecutor, in the light of information contained in the denunciation, will decide on the advisability of prosecution.

In all states it is acknowledged that the injured party may lodge a complaint so as to inform the competent authorities that an offence liable to penal sanctions has been committed. Considering that copyright offences affect a private interest, a number of countries make the exercise of public action conditional on the lodging of a complaint by the injured party. There is no doubt that the person mainly concerned is the author during his lifetime and thereafter his heirs until the end of the term of exclusive enjoyment of copyright granted to them under the law. There is even acknowledged to exist a prima facie presumption so as to permit prompt identification of the author. In most countries, this presumption operates to the benefit of the person whose name appears on the work or on the registration certificate when such a formality has to be complied with.

In the case of anonymous works and in order to respect the author's desire for anonymity, it is the publisher who represents the author. In certain countries with registration systems, the person whose name is registered represents the author, not only as regards anonymous works but also as regards pseudonymous works. These persons may thus lodge a complaint on behalf of the author in his stead.

When the work originates from several authors, countries whose legislation makes provision for this matter lay down in principle that each of the co-authors may institute proceedings individually. Each is thus able to lodge an individual complaint. It would seem that this also applies by way of jurisprudence in countries whose legislation contains no provision on this subject.

If the author or his heirs have assigned the exclusive rights to a third party, it is generally the assignee who is qualified to uphold and assert these rights and thus to bring an action. In Anglo-Saxon countries, this principle is complicated by procedural systems that draw a distinction between assignees and licensees (see Chapter 8).

In certain states, societies, bureaux, offices or professional associations of authors—that is, bodies set up to uphold authors' rights in relation to users and defend their members' material and moral interests—may lodge complaints in the event of an offence against literary property. On this subject, the solutions adopted vary tremendously from code to code, from law to law and from one set of regulations to another. This approach is sometimes followed in relation to international infringement when authors' societies have agreed among themselves to undertake to prosecute unlawful exploitation on their own territory of works belonging to members of authors' societies in other countries.

Some countries also accept that actions in respect of infringement of authors' rights should be lodged by the state of which the injured party is a national. Most states exclude this possibility, however.

Who entertains complaints?

Authorities competent to entertain complaints or denunciations vary considerably from one country to another. In most cases, however, jurisdiction is vested in a judicial authority. The complaint or denunciation is lodged either in the public prosecutor's office or directly with the competent court. The police authorities may also be empowered to receive complaints and denunciations dealing with copyright. More often than not the natural or legal person with a cause for action is free to choose from among the bodies provided under the law. On some occasions, the choice of the competent authority is determined by the nature of the offence.

What are the measures to punish breaches of copyright?

Practically all national legislations contain provisions that lay down the various measures to be applied in the event of copyright infringement. These provisions are, as a rule, scattered through a variety of legislative texts, national copyright legislation and criminal codes. Their purpose is to punish the offender and to compensate the injured party for the injury sustained. Action against innocent infringement, in cases where the infringer was not aware that he was breaking the law, is generally limited to stopping the infringing action and requiring confiscation of infringing copies. The legislation of each of the states that provide sanctions for breach of copyright inflicts upon those committing the breach principal penalties in the form of a fine or imprisonment or both. As a rule, these deterrent penalties are supplemented by measures whose purpose is to secure a just and adequate compensation for the injured person and to restore the status quo ante (the situation before the infringement).

Can punishment include fines and prison terms?

All legislations providing for sanctions in the event of copyright offences inflict cash fines on the offender for having perpetrated the offence. Culpable intent or wilful infringement is required by most laws before penalties can be imposed. Thus, if a person is found to have acted in good faith, he cannot be fined.

The amount of the fine may vary with the nature of the offence. Recent laws, however, show a clear trend towards a uniform rate for infringements.

The penalty of imprisonment, on the contrary, is not universally accepted. The rule would appear to be that, when it is provided, imprisonment is reserved for repeated offenders, the first offence attracting only a fine. Some legislations inflict both a fine and imprisonment on first offenders or either or both of these penalties at the discretion of the judge.

Are reparations provided for?

Many states grant to the copyright holder who has been the victim of a breach of his rights certain forms of assistance, this assistance being additional to the penalties inflicted on the perpetrator of the breach. Such assistance consists primarily of measures designed to provide a fair and adequate reparation for the material injury he has suffered. This normally involves confiscation of infringing copies or profits from the unlawful reproduction or performance as well as of any equipment specially provided for the unlawful reproduction. Authors may also be awarded additional monetary compensation.

All legislations practically without exception provide for the confiscation of infringing copies and the equipment used to manufacture them (plates, presses, moulds, matrices, photographs). They provide less frequently for the confiscation of receipts accruing from the unlawful reproduction or performance.

Are monetary awards made to victims?

Authors may obtain a compensation which in civil litigation takes the form of damages. In certain countries this form of assistance for the benefit of injured parties is expressly provided for in legislation. In determining the amount of damages, copyright laws either refer to the general rules of law or they may contain special rules on the subject. They may, for example, provide that the amount of damages (compensation) will be measured by the injury suffered by the owner of the right or the profits of the infringer. Some laws specify the amount or a minimum the court must award for infringement of certain rights.

Are there preventive measures?

In order to provide copyright holders with more effective protection, some legislations also contain preventive provisions designed to avoid infringements or halt them. These involve suits for the purpose of inducing a person to refrain from a given course of action, including injunctions calling for cessation of the offending act. Although prohibition is the most effective remedy against unlawful performance, there is another remedy for offences relating to material objects such as books, drawings and records. This remedy is the attachment of the objects or equipment used for its manufacture. Warrants for attachment are designed to facilitate the confiscation of infringing material and the proof of the commission of the offence pending determination of the case by the courts. Attachment is not an end in itself but a remedy to be confirmed or otherwise by the competent civil or penal court.

Certain countries have also enacted provisions of an administrative nature whereby officials can forbid the import of infringing works or bring about suspension of the sale or public performance of such works.

Is moral injury remedied?

Since a literary work is the expression and the projection of the writer's personality, offences against literary property may cause the author moral injury. Some legislations expressly recognize this and grant to the injured author the right to claim additional compensation or damages from the courts for the moral damage resulting from the offence. Authors are not generally able to secure monetary reparation for moral damages but provisions are often made for the text of the judgement handed down by the courts to be printed either in posters or newspapers. The cost of such publication is borne by the person or persons convicted.

12

International copyright

What are the origins of international protection?

The historic evolution of means of communication provides the basic explanation of how copyright protection has become increasingly international. Countries that adopted copyright laws originally were thinking primarily in terms of national uses and protection for works of the mind because the technologies of communication and the commercial markets for their products were limited. Countries protected works created and produced within their own territory. Not much thought was given to foreign works and national copyright laws had no effect in other countries until about a hundred years ago.

This situation began to change towards the end of the nineteenth century with the growth of an international book market. Then came the technological revolution that brought photography, cinematography, sound recording and broadcasting. The market for copyrighted works became greatly enlarged on the national and international levels as diffusion across national boundaries became more rapid and widespread. The need for international protection was recognized and governments moved more vigorously to secure protection for national works in foreign countries.

Is international protection possible without treaties?

Certain countries grant protection to works originating in other countries without the existence of an international treaty. They are entitled to take this step on their own and some have provided protection under their domestic laws not only to works of their own nationals but to those of the nationals of other countries. In the past, such protection was usually granted on the basis of reciprocity. One country would protect the works of another if the other country granted similar protection to its national works. Recently, more countries have taken the unilateral decision to grant protection to foreign works without insisting on reciprocity. The extension of national statutes to foreign works without regard to reciprocity simplifies copyright relations but is not yet the general rule.

Are there copyright treaties?

With the development of communications and recognition that authors must be assured protection of their rights in other countries, various kinds of international agreements were signed. These have taken the form of bilateral and regional treaties and multilateral or international treaties or conventions.

The first international copyright treaties were bilateral: that is, only two countries were involved. They usually provided that each state would provide the same protection to the authors of the other that they granted to their own authors. This practice is called 'national treatment'. In order to provide international protection via this route it is necessary to negotiate many treaties. Because of the obvious difficulty of securing worldwide copyright protection through the conclusion of bilateral treaties, they gradually became a rarity as more and more countries turned to regional and multilateral conventions.

Are there regional conventions?

Towards the end of the nineteenth century the countries of the Americas forged a number of regional copyright conventions. The Pan-American Conventions included the Montevideo Convention of 1889, the Mexico City Convention of 1902, the Rio de Janeiro Convention of 1906, the Buenos Aires Convention of 1910, the Caracas Agreement of 1911, the Havana Convention of 1928 and the Washington Convention of 1946. But the imperatives of the growing internationalization of communications made it apparent that regional conventions did not meet the need for universal protection.

How have the multilateral conventions evolved?

At the end of the nineteenth century, the first bilateral agreements and regional treaties came into existence and the first multilateral convention was established under pressure from European authors and publishers who felt the need for greater protection as an incentive to productivity and a growing commerce in protected works. This first multilateral agreement, concluded in 1886, was the Berne Convention for the Protection of Literary and Artistic Works. Any country of the world willing to grant the reciprocal protection established under the Berne Convention was free to adhere. What the Convention did essentially was to assimilate to the national repertory of each member state the works of each other member state. Protection is granted without observance of any formalities. Many times revised, the Convention had seventy-two contracting states by 1981.

What is the origin of the Universal Copyright Convention?

Prior to the Second World War the various states were either party to Berne, one or more of the Pan-American Conventions or had not acceded to any system of international copyright protection. Some of these states had also established bilateral agreements either through the conclusion of treaties or by proclamations. Beginning in 1928, however, attempts were made to unify international relations in the field of copyright.

During the period immediately following the Second World War, interest revived in broadening international protection so as to include certain countries, primarily of the Western Hemisphere which for various reasons had not joined Berne and had therefore held aloof from the international system of copyright protection. Unesco, heir to the Institute of Intellectual Cooperation of the League of Nations, which had already begun this work and with a commitment to facilitate access of all people to published materials, took up the task of developing a universal convention. The General Conference of Unesco at Mexico City in 1947 resolved that 'Unesco shall, with all possible speed and with due regard to existing agreements, consider the problem of improving copyright on a world-wide basis' (resolution 2.4.1). This resolution was confirmed at two subsequent sessions of the General Conference and the Secretariat of Unesco was instructed to prepare the draft of a convention to assure universal observance of copyright. Four committees of experts met between 1947 and 1951 to prepare the draft that was submitted to the Intergovernmental Copyright Conference convened in Geneva on 18 August 1952.

The Universal Copyright Convention was adopted by this conference not as a substitute for previously existing agreements but to establish a basis for protection among countries of widely differing cultural traditions sometimes with conflicting interests. The new convention, known commonly as UCC, with somewhat lower standards of protection than Berne, was to make it possible to establish treaty relations between the countries of the Berne Union[1] and those on the American continent. UCC was also intended to provide a system that would be acceptable to newly independent countries and those that had not yet come into the international copyright system. At the end of 1980, seventy-three states had either ratified or adhered to this convention.

One of the questions that was carefully considered when UCC was in the drafting stage and at the Geneva Conference of 1952 was the possible effect on the Berne Union. A safeguard clause was therefore adopted aimed at ensuring continued close observance of the Berne Convention.

---

1. Berne Union countries are those adhering to the original text of the Berne Convention or one of its revised texts.

What are the basic provisions of UCC and Berne?

Although these two international copyright conventions differ, certain fundamental rules ensure copyright protection to works originating in countries which are party to them. States that have ratified or acceded to either or both have an obligation to see that their domestic laws are in conformity with the convention binding them. It is possible, however, for national legislation to comply with convention principles in different ways and to work out voluntary or legislative solutions to such pressing contemporary questions as limits for photocopying.

Does the national treatment rule apply?

Common to both conventions is the fundamental principle of national treatment. According to this rule, works originating in a contracting state are protected in every other contracting state in the same manner as states protect works originating within their own territory. Stated in another way, works by a foreign author enjoy the same protection as the works of national authors. For example, a textbook first published in contracting State A will be protected in contracting State B in the same manner as State B protects a school text originating within its own territory. Published works are protected by the Berne Convention if they are first published in a Berne state and are protected under UCC if first published in a UCC-contracting state, or if their authors are nationals of a contracting state. Unpublished works are protected by each Convention if their authors are residents of a contractting State.

Is there minimum protection?

Both conventions provide for certain minimum conditions of protection. Scope and duration of protection as well as the question of formalities are covered. Each contracting state must respect these minimum conditions with regard to foreign works.

How is the scope of protection regarded?

The UCC contains few minimum conditions relating to the scope of the protection. Article I states: 'Each Contracting State undertakes to provide for the adequate and effective protection' of authors and other copyright holders. The rights were made more explicit in 1971 in Article IV*bis* to include the exclusive rights of reproduction, public performance and broadcasting. The states may implement these requirements through their national laws. The only specific minimum provision in UCC relates to the right of translation because of its international importance. Article V requires the authorization of the copyright holder of the original work. However, under certain conditions and after complying with certain formalities and the payment of royalties, authorization can be waived. The government of the country that wishes to publish the translation can grant a licence replacing authorization of the copyright owner when seven years have passed from the date of the first publication of the work and the work has not been translated into the national language or languages of the state where the applicant publisher resides.

Berne provides minimum conditions of protection for rights of reproduction, translation, public performance, recitation, broadcasting, cinematography, adaptation and recording of musical works. These rights are in principle exclusive rights but member states may regulate some of them as simple rights of remuneration under compulsory licences for broadcasting and sound recordings. The Berne Convention also recognizes the author's moral right to object to distortions, mutilation or other changes in his work that would be prejudicial to his honour or reputation.

How is duration of protection treated?

States are free to grant a longer term if they want, but accession to UCC requires them to provide a minimum term of protection of twenty-five years after the death of the author. States with a term calculated from the date of publication may preserve that system on condition that they observe a minimum of twenty-five years after publication.

In the case of Berne, states may provide a longer term but they are required to provide protection for a minimum period of fifty years after the death of the author. The rights of translation may be reduced to ten years calculated from the first publication in the original language if no translation has been published in the national language of the requesting country.

How about formalities?

The Berne Convention expressly provides that protection shall not be subject to any formalities. Under UCC, if a state requires compliance with any formalities, as a condition for protection, such formalities will be considered accomplished if all published copies of the work bear a copyright notice.

13

Copyright and
the developing world

Do developing countries have an interest in copyright?

Improvement of living conditions everywhere depends to a large extent on
the progress of education, science and culture. Such progress is made possible
through the dissemination of information and knowledge and its application to national development. Intellectual production is just as important
to the process of nation-building as material production, providing as it does
the foundation for all advancement. Every developing country today faces
the challenge of how to stimulate national production and gain full access
to worldwide resources of knowledge. These developments have placed great
pressures on educational institutions and creative communities everywhere.

A variety of measures are being taken by developing countries, including
the national production of books and other educational and cultural
products and development of modern communications, to achieve these
goals. These countries are also attempting to create a favourable climate for
national intellectual production and a fruitful exchange between nations.
No law or decree can produce these development goals, but the great
majority of states have found that a system of national and international
copyright law creates a climate in which the arts and sciences can flourish.

What is the role of copyright in development?

Young countries are anxious to have access to the best works of other nations
and to export their own. They must therefore protect their own authors and
provide them with the same guarantees as others. By protecting expressions
of the human mind, copyright enables countries to communicate their as-
pirations, ideas and accomplishments to the entire world. Copyright has a
critical impact on the flow of literary, scientific, musical and artistic works,
information and culture from one country to another. All countries therefore
have an interest in copyright. The regulation of copyright is consequently a
major task facing developing countries.

Developing countries have special needs that relate directly to copyright. They need easy access to copyrighted works via, among other means, radio as a major teaching tool. Some are preparing inventories of their cultural heritage and are seeking to provide support for artists and their works. As consumers of literary and artistic works, it is sometimes difficult to harmonize the needs of developing countries for access to these works with the demands of producer countries. The question is therefore posed as to how authors can be protected while meeting consumer demands in developing countries with limited financial resources.

The enactment of national copyright legislation does not automatically bring about the desired results. Public education to explain their rights to those affected is necessary to make the system work. Authors' societies can play an important role in implementation of copyright laws. National authorities must mobilize behind the creation of effective copyright administrative bodies. More benefits can accrue from joining the international copyright system through adherence to one or both of the two major international conventions.

Do developing countries have special needs?

During the post Second World War period, the needs of developing countries for educational materials have grown with the rising expectations of people everywhere. Unesco has taken the position that, whenever possible, a local edition of an educational work should be produced in developing countries at a selling price equal or less than that of an edition of the same work published in another country either by means of co-production agreements or by virtue of an authorization to reproduce. This procedure has been regarded as preferable to importing works published in the major producer nations.

In the 1960s, developing countries under great pressure to meet the educational needs of their people found that they were having difficulty obtaining rights to translate and reproduce needed educational materials. The needs of these countries were brought to the attention of the publishing countries where the rights were held. Developing countries needed access to university texts and other materials in local languages that were not available on the market and in less expensive editions than those exported from the industrialized countries. Their representatives said that copyright was blocking access to translation and reproduction of such works. The copyright owners, authors and publishers in the major publishing nations countered that authors were entitled to a fair return for their work and that their rights should be respected.

How did developing countries press their demands?

As a result of pressures brought to bear by developing countries, meetings of international copyright experts were held—the first in 1963 at Brazzaville.

Representatives of developing nations urged revision of copyright laws and the international conventions to oblige authors to release their rights for educational purposes in the developing world subject to payment of reasonable fees. Many African and Asian nations joined in making demands that culminated in a proposed change in the Berne Convention to enable developing countries to gain easier access to needed works. A Protocol to this effect was proposed by these developing countries at the 1967 meeting of the Intellectual Property Conference at Stockholm. Among the provisions of this protocol was the possibility of waiving copyright restrictions in respect to works required 'exclusively for teaching, study and research in all fields of education' if the author was given a compensation which conforms to 'standards of payment made to national authors'. It would also have permitted export of such editions among developing countries.

The idea of revising the Universal Copyright Convention was first raised by the General Conference of Unesco at its fourteenth session (Paris, 1966). After noting that 'the conventions . . . governing international relations in the matter of copyright should be partially revised to take account of the economic, social and cultural conditions obtaining in the developing countries . . .' and that Unesco should '. . . facilitate the accession . . . to the Universal Copyright Convention, so as to guarantee a minimum degree of protection to authors of works of the mind while allowing of a broad dissemination of culture', the General Conference unanimously adopted a resolution (14C/5.122) in which the Director-General of Unesco was invited to submit the matter as soon as possible to the competent bodies (primarily the Intergovernmental Copyright Committee)[1] so that they could examine the possibility of revising that instrument to benefit the developing countries.

How were the demands of the developing countries met?

The major publishing nations recognized the needs of developing countries for inexpensive textbooks and measures that would enable them to publish such editions. But they regarded the proposals of Stockholm as too drastic and refused to go along with them. The conflict endangered the very existence of the international copyright system, according to the major publishing nations. They sought solutions that would preserve authors' exclusive rights while providing machinery to ease the granting of rights for bona fide educational purposes. A joint study group composed of representatives of member states of both UCC and Berne suggested in 1969 that revisions of both instruments could be made that would accomplish this objective. The recommendations of this group were considered at a series of international

---

1. The Intergovernmental Copyright Committee was established by Article XI of the Universal Copyright Convention to study the problems concerning the application and operation of the Convention.

meetings and led to the conferences of 1971 where revisions of both conventions favouring developing countries were adopted.

What were the Paris revisions of 1971?

The revision conferences held in Paris to revise both conventions proposed that a limited compulsory licensing system be adopted for translation and reproduction of literary, scientific or artistic works needed by developing countries. This is the essence of what was finally adopted in the parallel revision sessions in Paris. It was a compromise solution designed to provide the basis for the granting of compulsory licences to translate or reproduce works published in developed countries for use in developing countries when a voluntary licence cannot be obtained. When the requisite number of states ratified or acceded to the revisions, on 10 July 1974 in the case of UCC and on 10 October 1974, for Berne, the convention revisions came into force applicable between states party to the revised conventions.

What was the general nature of the Paris revisions?

The general idea of these convention changes in favour of developing nations was to prevent them from being blocked in gaining access to materials needed for educational purposes. The compulsory licences may not be granted until the developing nation's publisher exhausts the normal methods for locating the copyright holder of the original work and normal business negotiations break down. Books may not be translated or reproduced for profitable sales. Books thus produced must be printed in the developing country and not exported to other countries except under specific conditions. If the original publisher publishes an edition of the book in the local language or in the original language for sale in the developing country at prices close to those paid for such works in the developing country, compulsory licences may not be granted. The amount of time allowed to the original publisher to produce such an edition differs with the category of work as noted below. There are also certain notification provisions—first to the original publisher if, after due diligence on the part of the applicant for a compulsory licence, he was not able to locate the publisher whose name appears on the work—then to national or regional copyright information centres or, as regards UCC, if none exists, to Unesco's International Copyright Information Centre.

What are the conditions for a licence for translation?

A translation licence may be obtained on the expiry of a period of three years from the first publication of a work if it is in a language in general use in one or more developed countries. Only one year must elapse in case of a translation into a vernacular language. A developing country can, however, with the unanimous consent of the developed countries party to the instrument (and subject to the condition that the language is not English, French or Spanish) translate into a language in general use one year after publication.

What are the characteristics of translation licences?

Each translation licence is non-exclusive and limited to teaching, scholarship or research. According to the revision conferences, the word 'scholarship' refers not only to instructional activities at all levels in tutorial institutions, primary and secondary schools, colleges and universities but also to a wide range of organized educational activities devoted to study of any subject. The word 'research' cannot be interpreted to permit the translation of copyrighted works by industrial research institutes or by private corporations doing research for commercial purposes.

Are there other conditions for translations?

The licence is subject to certain formal conditions and provides for an equitable compensation conforming to the scale of royalties normally paid for freely negotiated licences. This compensation should be paid in internationally convertible currency.

Furthermore, as regards works consisting mainly of illustrations, a licence for translation of the text and reproduction of the illustrations cannot be granted unless the conditions laid down for the reproduction are also fulfilled. Domestic legislation must also ensure an accurate translation of the work.

What are the conditions for broadcast translations?

The licence originally intended only for graphic publishers was extended by the revision conferences to broadcasting organizations with headquarters situated in a developing country subject to the following conditions: that the translation is made from a copy which has been produced and acquired in conformity with the laws of the state which granted the licence; that the sole aim of the translation is use in broadcasts destined exclusively for 'teaching' or 'the dissemination of the results of specialized technical or scientific research to experts in a particular profession'; that the translation and the broadcast are intended for an audience on the territory of the licensing state either 'live' or effected 'through the medium of sound or visual recording' accomplished legally and exclusively for the approved purposes; that under no circumstances are these recordings to be sent beyond the frontiers of the country or sold, rented or licensed within the country; that all uses of the translation are 'without any commercial purpose'.

A licence may equally be granted under the same conditions for the translation of 'any text incorporated in an audio-visual fixation which was itself prepared and published for the sole purpose of being used in connection with systematic instructional materials'.

What about reproduction licences?

A system of licences for reproduction was established in favour of the developing states. The licence may be issued on expiration of the five-year period of exclusivity, beginning on the date of the first publication of a particular edition of a work, so long as, in the developing country concerned, copies of that edition have not been distributed by the owner of the right of reproduction or with his authorization to the general public, or in connection with systematic instructional activities at a price comparable to that normally charged in that state for similar works, or if, during a period of six months, no authorized copy of the particular edition has been distributed in the state in the conditions stated above. The five-year period is reduced to three years for works of the natural and physical sciences and technology and increased to seven years for works of fiction, poetry, drama, music and art books.

A licence granted in the above conditions is non-exclusive, non-transferable, restricted to the needs of systematic instructional activities and intended for publication at the same price reasonably related to that normally charged in the concerned developing state for comparable works or at a lower price.

As in the case of a licence for translation, the licence for reproduction provides for just compensation conforming to the scale of royalties normally paid for freely negotiated licences. This compensation should be paid and transmitted in internationally convertible currency. An accurate reproduction must also be ensured to protect the moral and titular rights of the author.

The licences granted under this system, in principle, cover printed editions of literary, scientific or artistic works. However, a licence may also be obtained for audio-visual works prepared and published for the sole purpose of being used in connection with systematic instructional activities.

Are exports of translations and reproductions permitted?

The general principle is that copies produced in accordance with a licence for translation or reproduction cannot be exported. Nevertheless, this general prohibition appeared to the conferences for revision of the international conventions in 1971 as too harsh to the extent that it prohibits a licence holder from making an imprint or reproduction in a country other than the developing country for which the licence has been granted. In developing countries which do not have the infrastructure to ensure such reproduction, the imprint can take place outside the national territory where the following circumstances are met:

The contracting state which grants the licence does not possess within the territory, the means of imprint or reproduction, or, if these means exist, it cannot, for economic or practical reasons, ensure the reproduction of copies.

The country where the work of reproduction is effected is party to the Universal Copyright Convention or is a member of the Berne Union.

All the produced copies are sent to the licence holder in a dispatch of one or more packets for exclusive distribution in the country of the said licence holder. Furthermore, the contract between the licence holder and the establishment which does the reproduction should stipulate that the work of reproduction is lawful in the country where it is undertaken.

The licence holder does not entrust the work of reproduction to an establishment specially created for the reproduction of copies of works for which a licence has been granted.

The prohibition on export does not apply when a government organization or any public organization of a state which has been granted a licence sends the copies of a translation to another country if: the translation is not in English, French or Spanish; the recipients are nationals of the contracting country which issued the licence or the organizations grouping such nationals; the copies are utilized exclusively for teaching, scholarship or research; the distribution of the copies is non-commercial; and the country to which the copies are sent has given permission.